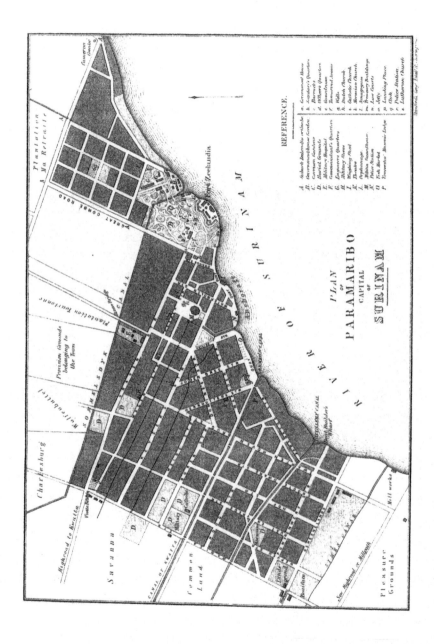

PLAN
OF
PARAMARIBO
CAPITAL
OF
SURINAM

REFERENCE.

A. Roberts Zedenbergweiche   a. Government House
B. Governmentshouse Garden   b. Secretary's Quarters
C. Garrison Gardens   c. Barracks
D. Harriet Grounds   d. Officers Quarters
E. Military Hospital   e. Guardroom
F. Commandant's Quarters   f. Bonaventul Avenue
G. Engineers Quarters   g. Wells
H. Military Store   h. Dutch Church
I. Weighing Shed   i. Catholic Church
K. Theatre   k. Moravian Church
L. Orphanage   l. Synagogues
M. Roman Guardhouse   m. Treasury Buildings
N. Police Station   n. Law Courts
O. Fish Market   o. Jetty
P. Venantius Masonic Lodge   p. Landing Place
                              q. Club
                              r. Police Station
                              s. Lutheran Church

RIVER OF SURINAM

Dutch Colonists
in the Americas
1615–1815

by
David Dobson

CLEARFIELD

Printed for
Clearfield Company by
Genealogical Publishing Co.
Baltimore, Maryland
2008

ISBN-13: 978-0-8063-5371-5
ISBN-10: 0-8063-5371-6

Made in the United States of America

Cover illustration: De Vries in East River

INTRODUCTION

By the late sixteenth century the Dutch were rapidly becoming the dominant maritime power in north-west Europe. Their ships, which initially were found trading throughout the North Sea, the Baltic Sea and the Bay of Biscay, soon began to expand their sphere of activity to include the Mediterranean, the Atlantic, later the Indian Ocean and beyond.

For 80 years the Dutch were engaged in a mighty struggle with Spain to win their independence, which was eventually achieved in 1648. This struggle increasingly began to include raids on Spanish shipping and settlements in the Caribbean. Their presence in the Caribbean gradually led to them establishing settlements in what had been Spanish territory. The Dutch were not unique in this development as the English and the French also were so engaged. Among the islands settled by the Dutch were Curacao, Saba, St Martin, and St Eustatius. On the South American mainland they established colonies in what is now Brazil and Surinam. The economy of these settlements was the production of sugar, which had a very profitable market in Europe. Dutch links with North America commenced at a slightly later date with the voyage of Henry Hudson in 1609. By 1614 they were permanently settled on the Hudson River. Dutch operations in the Americas were under the aegis of the Dutch West India Company, which was founded in 1621 with a monopoly of trade with America and Africa. By the 1620s the New Netherlands colony along the Hudson River had developed an economy around Albany supplying furs to the European market, with an agricultural economy on the Lower Hudson Valley supplying foodstuffs for the Dutch West Indies. Later the Dutch absorbed the small Swedish colony on the Delaware into their New Netherlands colony.

However, in 1664 the English invaded the New
Netherlands and added it to their burgeoning empire.

Thousands of Netherlanders had settled in the Americas
during the seventeenth and eighteenth centuries. Their
records pertaining to what is now New York have long
been available to their descendants seeking their roots.
However, there are additional records in Europe, mostly
in archives in London, Rotterdam, and Amsterdam,
which are not generally available to researchers in North
America. This book is based on such records and
identifies early Dutch settlers and some of their
descendants, also a few early shipping links, in the
Americas between 1615 and 1815.

David Dobson
St Andrews, Scotland.

SOME SHIPPING LINKS

De Blauwe Duif, master Jan Jansen Bestevaer, from the Texel,
    North Holland, bound for the New Netherlands in 1656.
    [NSMA]

De Blauwen Haen, master Cornelis Oldemarckt, from
    Amsterdam bound for the New Netherlands in 1644.
    [NSMA]

De Brandaris, from Amsterdam to the New Netherlands in
    September 1641. [NSMA]

De Branderburg, master Jan Cornelissen Kuyper, from Fort
    Kyck on the Rio Essequibo to Middleburg, Zealand, in
    August 1700. [SPAWI.1700/715]

De Jonge Jan en Theodore, master Jan Reygers, from Surinam
    to Amsterdam, but captured by HMS Hyena on 6 March
    1782. [PCCol.1766-1783.461]

De Leeuwinne, 100 lasts, Vice Admiral Jan Pieterszoon, from
    Flushing, Zeeland, on 22 January 1627 bound via the
    Canary Islands and the coast of Africa to the Amazon to
    settle on the River Wiapoco. [HS.series II, Vol.171/269]

De Liefde, master Meyndart Janszoon Schellinger, at Barbados
    in 1640. [GAR.ONA.138.422.645]

De Schildtpad, Captain Eelckens, from Amsterdam to America
    in 1616. [GAA.na#645/36-43]

De Vlieghenden Draeck, master Galeyn van Stapels, from
    Flushing, Zeeland, on 22 January 1627 bound via the
    Canary Islands and the coast of Africa to the Amazon to
    settle on the River Wiapoco. [HS.series II, Vol.171/269]

De Vruntschap, master James Moorcock, at Barbados and St
    Kitts in 1644. [GAR.ONA.95.235.385]

King Charles, from the Texel to New York in 1668.
    [PCCol.1668/496]

Matthew and Francis of London, 300 tons, master Richard
      Bread, from the Texel to Barbados in 1668.
      [PCCol.1668/823]

Nieuw Jorck, from Amsterdam to New York in April 1668.
      [GAA#2845]

Prins Willem, from Amsterdam to the New Netherlands in
      1648. [NSMA]

Rensselaerwijk, master Jan Tjepkeszoon Schellinger, from the
      Texel in North Holland bound for the New Netherlands
      in 1636. [GAA#1045]

St Jan van Amsterdam, a privateer at Curacao in 1670.
      [ActsPCCol.1670/901-906]

Sarah and Mary, 270 tons, master Edward Burton jr., from the
      Texel to Barbados in 1668. [PCCol.1668/823]

Susannah of Amsterdam, when bound from Guinea to Curacao
      was captured by the English and taken to Jamaica in
      1679. [PCCol.1679/1321]

Ter Vere, 90 lasts, Captain Hendrick Jacobszoon Lucifer, from
      Flushing, Zeeland, on 22 January 1627 bound via the
      Canary Islands and the coast of Africa to the Amazon to
      settle on the River Wiapoco. [HS.series II, Vol.171/269]

Wapen van Dordrecht, master Jacob Corneliszoon, to Africa,
      Brasil, Barbados and the New Netherlands in 1640.
      [GAR.ONA.86.199.372]

REFERENCES

Archives

ARA =   Algemeen Rijkarchief s'Gravenhage
BA =   Barbados Archives
EUL =   Edinburgh University Library
GAA =   Gemeentarchief Amsterdam
GAR =   Gemeentarchief Rotterdam
NA =   National Archives, London
NAS =   National Archives of Scotland
NSMA =   Nederlands Scheepvaartmuseum Amsterdam
NWIC =   New West India Company
OAC =   Old Archive of Curacao
RAK =   National Archives, Copenhagen
SRO =   Surrey Record Office, England

Publications

GM   =   Gentleman's Magazine, series
HMC =   Historical Manuscripts Commission,
         [Report on American Manuscripts in the
         Royal Institution of Great Britain]
HS   =   Hayluyt Society publications, series
JCTP =   Journal of the Committee for Trade and the
         Plantations, series
PCCol=   Acts of the Privy Council, Colonial series
RAC =   Riches from Atlantic Commerce, [Leiden 2003]
SPAWI=   Calendar of State Papers, America and
         The West Indies, series
SPCol = Calendar of State Papers, Colonial, series

Earliest Picture of New Amsterdam.

A SURINAM PLANTER.
(From Stedman's "Surinam.")

DUTCH COLONISTS IN THE AMERICAS 1615-1815

ABBENSETZ, ..., a member of the Council of Berbice, 1763.

ABEEL, JOHANNES, a resident of Albany, New York, in 1700; Recorder of Albany, 1702; Commissioner for Indian Affairs, 1708. [SPAWI.1700/845; 1702/999; 1702-03/29, 748; 1708/621]

ACKERDYK, PIETER, from Rotterdam, an employee of the Dutch West India Company at Fort Kyck, Overal, Rio Essequibo, returned to the Netherlands aboard the Brandenburg in 1700. [SPAWI.1700.715]

ACKERMAN, CORNELIUS, from Hackensack, Bergen County, New Jersey, husband of Elizabeth Van Vorheasen, a Loyalist soldier, died in Shelburne, Nova Scotia, pre 1786. [NA.AO13.25.495][HMC.A.IV/344]

ACKERMAN, JACOBUS, in Hackensack, New Jersey, 1768. [see NA.AO13.25.9]

ACKERMAN, JOHANNES, son of Johannis Ackerman, formerly a farmer in Franklin, Bergen County, New Jersey, a Lieutenant of Militia, in Greenwich, petitioned the Commander in Chief on 5 December 1779; a refugee in New York, petitioned Governor William Tryon on 1 February 1780; petitioned Governor William Franklin on 5 May 1780, settled in Shelburne, Nova Scotia, by 1786. [HMC.A.II/70, 85, 118][NA.AO13.25.1]

ACKERMAN, PETER, from Hackensack, New Jersey, a Loyalist in 1776, a refugee, petitioned Sir Henry Clinton on 30 November 1779, settled in Shelburne, Nova Scotia, by 1786. [HMC.A.II/68][NA.AO13.25.5]

ACKERMAN, RICHARD, formerly in Hackensack, Bergen County, New Jersey, who settled in Shelburne, Nova Scotia, by 1786. [see NA.AO13.19.363; AO13.25.9]

ACKERMAN, WILLIAM, from Stillwater, Albany County, New York, a Loyalist who settled in Sorel, Canada, by 1786. [NA.AO12.110.13]

ACKERSON, GARRET JACOB, formerly of Tappan, Orange County, New York, a Loyalist who settled in Cornwallis, Nova Scotia, by 1786. [NA.AO13.26.3]

ADOLF, PIETER, in New York, 1690. [SPAWI.1690/954]

ADRIAANSON, PIETER, Governor of St Eustatius, 1665. [SPAWI.1665.1042]

ADRIAENSZOON, PIETER, from Flushing, Zealand, on the Golden Cock of Flushing with settlers to Brazil in 1616.[HS.2nd series, vol.171/163]

AERNOUTSZOON, Captain JURRIAEN, in Acadia, 1674.

AERTSEN, GARRET, in New York, 1702. [SPAWI.1702/1206]

AERTSZOON, GOVERT, a merchant, to the New Netherlands aboard the St Jacob, master Haye Janszoon, in 1646. [GAA.NA#734B/80]

ALBERT, HENDRICK, member of the crew of Captain Kidd's ship the Adventure 1696. [SPAWI.1700/354]

ALBERTS, WYNTIE, was granted land in New York, 1686. [SPAWI.1686/952]

ALBERTSEN, ALBERT, a shipmaster at Barbados, 1655. [SPAWI.1655/1973]

ALBERTSZOON, HENDRICK, a baker in the New Netherlands, 1639. [GAA.NA#1054/60]

ANDRIESSEN, CHRISTIAAN, master of the Meeuw at Surinam, 1793. [NWIC]

APLE, JOHANNES, a resident of Albany, New York, in 1702.[SPAWI.1702/999]

ARENTS, JACOB, and his three children in New Jersey, naturalised there in 1716. [JCTP.Vol.V/35]

ARNSE, SAMUEL, a resident of Albany, New York, in 1702.[SPAWI.1702/999]

BACKER, ALBERTUS, Commander of Essequibo in 1789.

BAKKER, JOHANNES, master of the Aurora at Surinam, 1772, 1775. [NWIC]

BAKKERBENE, HENDRICK JANSZOON, a merchant, to the New Netherlands aboard the St Jacob, master Haye Janszoon, in 1646. [GAA.NA#734B/80]

BALCK, JACOB, petitioned the Council of New York in 1702. [SPAWI.1702/241]

BANCKER, EVERT, a resident of Albany, New York, in 1702; Commissioner for Indian Affairs, 1708; 1720; 1731. [SPAWI.1702/999; 1708/621; 1720/230; 1731/478]

BANTA, CORNELIUS, of Hackensack, New Jersey, 1783. [NA.AO12.110.29]

BANTA, GARRET, of Bergen, New Jersey, 1783. [NA.AO12.110.19]

BANTA, JACOB, of New Jersey, 1783. [NA.AO12.110.25]

BANTA, PETER, of New Jersey, 1783. [NA.AO12.110.25]

BANTA, SIEBA, of New Jersey, 1783. [NA.AO12.110.23]

BANTA, WEART, a carpenter and refugee from Hackinsack, New Jersey, a Lieutenant of the King's Militia

Volunteers, petitioned William Tryon, Captain General and Governor of New York, on 7 March 1780; settled in Shelburne, Nova Scotia, by 1783. [HMC.A.II/98][NA.AO12.15.200]

BARBE, ADRIAN, a Walloon dyer, with his wife and four children, to emigrate to Virginia 1621. (?). [SPCol.1574-1660:498]

BARRENTSZOON, HERMAN, a shipmaster at Barbados, 1655. [SPAWI.1655/1973]

BARRI, JACOBUS, Governor of St Martin's, 1734. [SPAWI.XLI.592]

BATE, JODOCUS, on the River Essequibo, clerk of the Dutch West India Company, 1700. [SPAWI.1700.690]

BATTARIE, PIETER, Commander of St Eustatius, 1680. [SPAWI.1680/1358]

BAUER, CASPAR, from Schoharie, Tryon County, New York, settled in New Brunswick by 1786. [NA.AO13.80.44]

BAYARD, NICOLAS, in New York, 1689, 1702, 1703. [SPAWI.1689/665, 667; 1702-03/29, 224, etc]

BAYER, BASTIAEN OTTO, in Antigua, 1709. [SPAWI.1709/443]

BAYER, JNO. OTTO, in Antigua, 1709. [SPAWI.1709/443]

BECK, ABRAHAM, Governor of Curacao, 1708 to 1710.

BECK, JACOB, Governor of Curacao, 1704 to 1708. [NWIC#201/163]

BECK, MATTHIAS, Vice-Governor of Curacao from 1655 to 1664.

BECKMAN, GERARD, in King's County, New York, 1689, 1703; Councillor of New York, dead by 1725.

[SPAWI.1689/352; 1703/29, 100][JCTP.BB/81]
[PCCol.1720-1745.833]

BECKMAN, HENRY, in Marble Town, Ulster County, New
York, 1719. [JCTP.Vol.V/221]

BEDLOO, WILLEM, a captain of militia in Surinam, 1730s

BEECHER, JOHANNES, a member of the House of
Representatives of New York, 1701.
[SPAWI.1701/1117]

BEECKMAN, GERARDUS, was pardoned by the Privy
Council, Colonial, on 7 April 1692; Councillor of New
York, 1723; died 1724. [PCCol.1680-1720.204]
[SPAWI.1723/606; 1724/392]

BEECKMAN, JOHANNES, a resident of Albany, New York,
in 1700, 1702. [SPAWI.1700/845; 1702/999]

BEECKMAN, SAMUEL, an employee of the Dutch West
India Company at Fort Kyck, Overal, Rio Essequibo,
1700. [SPAWI.1700.715]

BEEKENKAMP, JACOB, master of the Paulus at Surinam,
1759. [NWIC]

BEEKER, FREDERICK, naturalised in New York, 1735.
[SPAWI.XLI.591]

BEEKMAN, ABRAHAM, Commander of Essequibo, 1680s -
1700. [SPAWI.1700/715]

BEEKMAN, GERARD JOHN, a merchant in New York in
1778. [NA.AO13.90.99]

BEEKMAN, Colonel HENRY, in New York, 1698, 1703.
[SPAWI.1698/593ii; 1703/29, 748]

BEEKMAN, SAMUEL, Commander of Essequibo, 1703, died
1707; at Fort Kyck Overal, Rio Essequibo, 1700, 1703.
[SPAWI.1700/715; 1702-03/151 etc].

BEEKS, WILLEM, Governor of Curacao in 1670. [PCCol.1670/906]

BEKER, JOHANNES, a resident of Albany, New York, in 1702.[SPAWI.1702/999]

BENTHERSE, BALTUS, a resident of Albany, New York, in 1702.[SPAWI.1702/999]

BENTHERSE, MARTER, a resident of Albany, New York, in 1702.[SPAWI.1702/999]

BERGH, ADAM, from Dutchess County, New York, settled in Shelburne, Nova Scotia, by 1786. [NA.AO13.26.39]

BERGH, CHRISTIAN, from Dutchess County, New York, settled in Shelburne, Nova Scotia, by 1786. [NA.AO13.26.42]

BERNAGIE, BASTIAAN, to Curacao as an employee of the Dutch New West India Company around 1682, Governor there from 1692 to his death in 1700.

BEST, CONRAD, son of Jacob Best, husband of Catherine …., from Hosick, Albany County, New York, a Loyalist soldier from 1777, both died in Canada. [NA.AO12.31.128]

BEST, HERMANUS, son of Jacob Best a farmer in Hosick, Albany County, New York, a Loyalist soldier who settled at Mississique Bay by 1786. [NA.AO12.26.167]

BEST, JACOB, in Hosick, Albany County, New York, father of Conrad, Hermanus, and Jacob, 1783. [NA.AO13.11.B2]

BEST, JACOB, a farmer from Hosick, Albany County, New York, a Loyalist soldier from 1777, died on Carlton Island, Canada, around 1782. [NA.AO13.11.B2]

BEYS, HENRICUS, a Dutch Reformed Church minister in New York who was excommunicated as he became an

Episcopalian, then DRC minister in Curacao from 1713 to his death in 1716. [NWIC#205/399]

BICKES, JACOB, a Dutch Reformed Church minister on St Croix, Danish West Indies, 1754. [RAK.WIC.429]

BINCKES, ..., Governor of Dutch Tobago in 1678. [PCCol.1678/1211, 1237]

BINKES, JACOB, at New York in 1673. [SPAWI.1673.1143]

BISCHOP, J. P., a planter at Aurora, Essequibo, before 1802. [NAS.RD3.298.262]

BLAAU, RICHARD, in New York 1746, died 1774. [see NA.AO13.63.410]

BLAAU, WALDRON, from New York city, Captain of the New Jersey Volunteers, died in St John, New Brunswick, on 18 October 1783. [NA.AO12.22.309]

BLANKER, GERRIT, at Fort William Henry, New York, 1700. [SPAWI.1700/702]

BLANKERTS, LEYSBERT, a Dutch inhabitant of New York, petitioned the Privy Council in 1668. [SPAWI.1668.1885]

BLASS, PETER, a farmer from Albany County, New York, a Loyalist who settled at Sorel, Canada, by 1788. [NA.AO12.64.300]

BLAUVELT, JOHN, of Bergen, New Jersey, 1783. [NA.AO12.110.85]

BLAUVELT, THEUNIS, a bricklayer from Orange township, Orange County, New York, a Loyalist soldier who settled on the Susket River, Shelburne County, Nova Scotia, by 1783. [NA.AO13.11.B2]

BLAUVELT, THUNIS, a Loyalist lieutenant of the King's Militia Volunteers, in New York, 1779; of Herringtown,

Bergen County, New Jersey, in London by 1784.
[NA.AO13.96.390][HMC.A.I/414]

BLEEKER, JACOBUS, in New Rochelle, New York, 1786.
[see NA.AO.T79.70.92]

BLEEKER, JANSE, Recorder of Albany, New York, in 1698,
1699. [SPAWI.1698/822ii; 1699/250]

BLEEKER, Captain JOHANNES, a messenger to the Indians
in New York, 1699; a resident of Albany in 1700; Mayor
of Albany, 1702; 1711. [SPAWI.1699/245; 1700/845;
1702/999; 1711/863]

BLEEKER, NICOLAS, Commissioner of Indian Affairs of
New York, at Albany in 1730. [SPAWI.1730/622]

BLOCK, HANS, residing on the Delaware River, 1664.
[SPAWI.1664.808]

BLOCKEMAKER, HARMEN PIETERSZOON, with his wife
Martije Jans, and daughter **Janetje** .... New
Netherlands

BLOCKX, HARMTJE, to the New Netherlands in 1664.
[GAA.NA.2292/111/51]

BLOM, JACOB, possibly a tradesman at Fort William Henry,
New York, in 1702. [SPAWI.1702/387]

BLOOM, AARON, blockmaker in New York, 1700.
[SPAWI.1700/951]

BLYCKER, JAN JANSE, was appointed a justice of the peace
for Albany, New York, on 27 May 1691.
[SPAWI.1691/1533]

BOELEM, JACOB, in New York, 1702. [SPAWI.1702/999]

BOER, JAN CORNELIUSSEN, from Flushing to Surinam on
the Schakerloo in 1668.
[SPAWI.1668.1746][PCCol.1668/769]

BOGAERT, JACOB, a resident of Albany, New York, in 1700. [SPAWI.1700/845]

BOGARDUS, CORNELIS, was appointed Sheriff of Ulster and Duchess Counties, New York, 19 March 1691; a resident of Albany in 1700, 1702. [SPAWI.1691/1366; 1700.845; 1702/99]

BOGART, GUISBERT, in Tappan, Orange County, New York, pre 1776. [see NA.AO12.64.221]

BOGART, JOHN, in New York, deceased by 1783. [NA.AO12.110.67]

BOLL, ..., secretary to the Governor of Surinam, 1671. [SPAWI.1671/486]

BOLLAERT, HERMAN, master of the <u>Neptunus</u> at Surinam, 1775. [NWIC]

BORGAT, WILLEMJE MYLDEN, a widow in New York, 1719. [JCTP.Vol.V/220]

BORN, JOHAN, a Dutch Reformed Church minister on St Thomas, 1737, husband of Maria, daughter of Isaac Runnels. [RAK.WIC.431]

BOSS, JACOB, naturalised in New York, 1735. [SPAWI.XLI.591]

BOTTELMAN, HENDRICK, an indentured servant in Barbados, 1645. [GAA.NA#1620]

BRANDT, JACOB, born 1644, died in Barbados on 20 June 1700, buried in St Michael's churchyard on 21 June 1700. [St Michael's burial register]

BRANDT, MARAIS, senior, probate 17 February 1671 Barbados. [BA.RB6/8/374]

BRANDT, MARCUS, a Commissioner of the States General in Surinam, 1676. [SPAWI.1676/943]

BRASIER, ABRAHAM, was pardoned by the Privy Council, Colonial, on 7 April 1692. [PCCol.1680-1720.204]

BRAT, AARON, probably in Tryon County, New York, in 1786. [see NA.AO123.14.48]

BRAT, ANTHONY, a resident of Albany, New York, in 1700, 1702. [SPAWI.1700/845; 1702/999]

BRAT, BARENT, a resident of Albany, New York, in 1702.[SPAWI.1702/999]

BRAT, DANIELL, a resident of Albany, New York, in 1700, 1702. [SPAWI.1700/845; 1702/999]

BRAT, JOHANNES, a resident of Albany, New York, in 1702.[SPAWI.1702/999]

BREAMS, HARMON BEERENS, in St George's parish, Barbados, probate 7 June 1671. [BA.RB6/8/224]

BREES, ANTHONY, a resident of Albany, New York, in 1702.[SPAWI.1702/999]

BREMER, CARL, master of the <u>Jonge Lambrecht</u> at Surinam, 1773. [NWIC]

BRIES, ANTHONY, a resident of Albany, New York, in 1700. [SPAWI.1700/845]

BRIGHTMIOR, CONRODE, naturalised in New York, 1735. [SPAWI.XLI.591]

BRINKERHOFF, HENDRICK, in Bergen Neck, New Jersey, 1783. [NA.AO13.87.93]

BRINKERHOOF, DERICK, in New York city, 1778. [NA.AO13.92.173]

BROCKEHAVEN, CHRISTIAN, in Barbados, probate 5 August 1656. [BA.RB6/13/141]

BROCKHOLES, ANTHONY, in New York, 1701.
[SPAWI.1701/871]

BROECK, WESSELTON, a resident of Albany, New York,
in 1702.[SPAWI.1702/999]

BROEN, MARCUS, Secretary of Surinam, 1680s

BROUWER, PIETER, introduced sugar to Barbados 1630s

BROWER, JACOB, from Bergen Point, New Jersey, a
Loyalist, settled in Digby, Nova Scotia, by 1786.
[NA.AO13.25.66]

BRUGMAN, ..., a planter in Curacao around 1719.

BRUMONT, FREDERICK, a witness in New Amsterdam,
Berbice, 1819. [NAS.RD5.167.185]

BRUN, MANUEL, a witness in Nevis, 1686.
[SPAWI.1686/678]

BRUYN, JACOBUS, in New York, 1735. [SPAWI.XLI.591]

BRUYN, JAN HENDEREK, a councillor of New York, 1685.
[SPAWI.1685/186]

BULLT, JAN, a Walloon laborer, with his wife and four
children, to emigrate to Virginia 1621. (?). [SPCol.1574-
1660:498]

BURGH, ALBERT COENRAETSZOON, on the South
River of the New Netherlands, 1629. [NSMA.VRBMS
letterbook]

BURMEESTER, GERRIT, an indentured servant in
Barbados, 1645. [GAA.NA#1620]

BUSH, JOHANNES, petitioned for land in Ulster County,
New York, in April 1702. [SPAWI.1702/351]

BYVANK, EVERT, a resident of Westchester, New York, in
1700. [SPAWI.1700/575]

BYVANK, EVERT, in New York, 1783. [HMC.A.IV/9]

CALLAERT, PIETER, a planter in Essequibo before 1772. [NWIC#301/133]

CAMBRON, THEODORUS, a Dutch Reformed Church minister in Curacao from 1714

CAMFORT, GERALDUS, a resident of Albany, New York, in 1702.[SPAWI.1702/999]

CAPPLEMAN, BARNARD, in Barbados, probate 10 July 1673. [BA.RB6/9/33]

CASTENSE, WARNER, a resident of Albany, New York, in 1702.[SPAWI.1702/999]

CHUYLER, JOHANNES, a resident of Albany, New York, in 1702.[SPAWI.1702/999]

CLAES, ANDRES, a resident of Albany, New York, in 1702.[SPAWI.1702/999]

CLAESEN, LAWRENCE, an interpreter at Albany, New York, in 1700. [SPAWI.1700/845]

CLAUSE, ARNOUT, a resident of Albany, New York, in 1702.[SPAWI.1702/999]

CLAVER, ADRIAEN, a privateer in the Caribbean, around 1700

CLEMENT, PERTER, a resident of Albany, New York, in 1702.[SPAWI.1702/999]

CLOCH, MARTIN, a prisoner in New York, 1702. [SPAWI.1702/999, 1166, 1199]

CLOOTS, PIETER, a Jesuit on Curacao around 1738.

CLOPPER, PETER, possibly in Nova Scotia, 3 May 1769.[PCCol.1766-1783.194]

COEL, CORNELIUS, in Ulster County, New York, 1719. [JCTP.Vol.V/222]

COERMAN, HERMAN, fiscal of Curacao, 1760s.

COERTEN, MYNDEXT, in King's County, New York, 1689; was pardoned by the Privy Council, Colonial, on 7 April 1692. [PCCol.1680-1720.204][SPAWI.1689/352]

COEYMAN, BARENDT, in Albany, New York, 1699. [SPAWI.1699/669]

COLLICKMAN, DENNIS, was naturalised in Maryland in 1702. [SPAWI.1702/242]

COMBE, NICOLAAS, a customs clerk and planter in Curacao, 1760s.

CONSTANT, PIETER, Governor of Tobago, 1672. [SPAWI.1672/995]

CORLAIRE, B., a resident of Albany, New York, in 1700. [SPAWI.1700/845]

CORNELLISSEN, DIRICK, a shipmaster in Jamaica, 1687. [SPAWI.1687/1286]

CORNELLISSEN, HENRICK, a shipmaster at Barbados, 1655. [SPAWI.1655/1973]

CORNELLISSEN, JACOB, member of the crew of Captain Kidd's ship the Adventure 1696. [SPAWI.1700/354]

CORNELLISSEN, JOHN, purchased land east of Huntington, Nassau Island Suffolk County, New York, 1702. [SPAWI.1702/364]

CORNELISSEN, MAES, a resident of Albany, New York, in 1700. [SPAWI.1700/845]

CORNELISSEN, Mrs, wife of Maes Cornellisen, a resident of New York or Albany, then in Amsterdam, successfully petitioned King Charles II for permission to return to New York from Amsterdam aboard the Fort Albany of New York in 1669. [SPAWI.1669.29]

CORNELISZOON, IJBRANT, to Brazil, 1617. [RAC#65]

CORTLAND, PHILIP, in New Jersey, 1741. [PCCol.1720-1745.834]

CORTLAND, PHILIP, eldest son and heir of Mary Walton Hughes, a tenant in New York city, 1771. [JCTP.Vol.78/225]

COSENS, BARNE, appointed as Clerk of the Council of New York from 1698; sworn as Clerk and Register of the High Court of Chancery of New York, 1701; 1703. [SPAWI.1698/855; 1700/953; 1701/584; 1702-03/340]

COSTER, ANTHONY, a resident of Albany, New York, in 1700. [SPAWI.1700/845]

COVENHOVEN, ROLEFF, born around 1700, possibly resident of Monmouth County, New Jersey, alive in 1783. [see NA.AO100.301]

COYMAN, THOMAS, son of James Coyman in Amsterdam, a merchant who was buried in St Michael's churchyard, Barbados, in 1660, probate 31 January 1660. [BA.RB6/14/381]

CREGIER, HENDRICKUS, member of the crew of Captain Kidd's ship the Adventure 1696. [SPAWI.1700/354]

CREUTZ, CAREL OTTO, an army lieutenant in Surinam, 1749.

CRINSENS, ABRAHAM, in Surinam, 1678. [PCCol.1678/1275]

CROMMELIN, WIGBOLD, Governor of Surinam, from 1753 to 1763. [NWIC]

CRUGER, HENRY, senior, formerly in New York, probate March 1780 PCC [NA.AO13.95.22]

CRUGER, JOHN, an Alderman of New York, 1727.
[SPAWI.1727/763v]

CRUGER, Lieutenant Colonel JOHN HARRIS, a merchant
in New York, also chamberlain and member of the
Counil of New York city, a Loyalist officer, from
Savannah to New York in 1783. [HMC.A.III/29, 369,
409][NA.AO12.20.296]

CRUGER, VALENTINE, deceased by 1703, his widow Jacob
(sic) Minor Cruger was executrix to Ouzel Van Swieten
in New York, probate January 1703 PCC

CRUTTER, PETER, naturalised in New York, 1735.
[SPAWI.XLI.591]

CRYSENS, ABRAHAM, a Dutch Admiral at Surinam, 1668.
[SPAWI.1668.1733]

CUYLER, ABRAHAM, Commissioner of Indian Affairs of
New York, at Albany in 1730. [SPAWI.1730/622]

CUYLER, ABRAHAM, late Mayor of Albany, New York, a
Loyalist in New York, 1782, [HMC.A.III/57, 90, 92]

CUYLER, CORNELIUS, merchant in Albany, New York,
1735. [SPAWI.XLI.591]

CUYLER, HENDRIK, an alderman of New York, 1687,
1689, 1690; a merchant in New York, 1712.
[SPAWI.1687.1424; 1689/352; 1690/780; 1712/433]

CUYLER, HENRY, a Loyalist in New York, 1782.
[HMC.A.III/94]

CUYLER, JOHANNES, a resident of Albany, New York, in
1700, 1702, Commissioner of Indian Affairs of New
York, at Albany in 1720, 1730.[SPAWI.1700/845;
1702/999; 1720/230; 1730/622]

DAMONT, JAN, a Walloon laborer, with his wife, to emigrate
to Virginia 1621. (?). [SPCol.1574-1660:498]

DANIELSE, ARENT a resident of Albany, New York, in 1702.[SPAWI.1702/999]

DANIELSE, JAN, a resident of Albany, New York, in 1702.[SPAWI.1702/999]

DANIELSE, SYMON, a resident of Albany, New York, in 1702.[SPAWI.1702/999]

DASSE, ALEXANDER, possibly from Amsterdam, probate 12 March 1666 Barbados. [BA.RB6/15/494]

DAVITS, METGE, aged 18 years, indented in Amsterdam as a servant for three years in the New Netherlands during 1656. [GAA.NA#1205/45]

DE BIJ, WILLEM, Commissioner of the Slave Trade in Curacao, 1714.

DE BOER, ADRIAEN, master of the Helena at Surinam, 1777. [NWIC]

DE BONG, CHRISTIAN, 1783. [NA.AO12.111.1]

DE BRUYNE, PIETER, emigrated from Flushing on 22 January 1627, settled on the River Wiapoco. [HS, 2nd series, vol.171]

DE BUCK, JAN SYMONSZOON, in St Eustatius, 1646. [GAR.ONA.334.110.289]

DECKER, ISAAC, from Decker's Ferry, Long Island, New York, a Loyalist officer from 1776, settled in Shelburne, Nova Scotia, by 1786. [NA.AO.13.24.111]

DE CLERQ, ISAAC, master of the Junge Ruyter at Surinam, 1772, 1774. [NWIC]

DE DECKER, JOHAN, supercargo on De Swarte Arent at New Amsterdam in 1655.[GAA]

DE DECKER, JOHN, a member of the Council of the New Netherlands in 1664. [SPAWI.1664.788]

DE HART, MATHYAT, master of the Unity, bound from Aberdeen, Scotland, to America on 13 November 1691. [NAS.E72.1.19]

DE DIEMER, ERNEST FREDERICK, fort major in Brooklyn, New York, in 1783. [HMC.A.IV/197, 296]

DE DIEMER, FREDERICK, Captain of the 60th [Royal American] Regiment, 24 June 1782. [HMC.A.II/539]

DE FEER, MATHIJS, Commander of Berbice, 1687.

DE GRAAFF, JOHANNES, Secretary of St Maarten, Commander there from 1775 to 1782 when he returned to the Netherlands.

DE GRUYTER, BALTASAR, a planter in St Eustatia, 1644. [GAR.MA#206/225/363]

DE HALS, ..., a physician to Bradenham the pirate, 1702. [SPAWI.1702/553]

DE HART, CORNELIUS, in New Jersey, 1749. [PCCol.1750/485]

DE HART, JOSEPH, in Elizabethtown, New Jersey, 1783. [HMC.A.IV/376]

DE HART, MATTHEW, in Maryland, 1698. [SPAWI.1698/

DE HEERE, JAN, of the Dutch West India Company at Fort Kyck, Overal, Rio Essequibo, 1700. [SPAWI.1700.715]

DE HEERE, LAURENS, Commander of Essequibo, from 1719 until his death in 1729

DE HEM, JACOB, died in Barbados on 1 March 1677. [Andrews Plantation gravestone]

DE JONG, JACOB PIETERSZOON, a planter in Essequibo, and in 1685 Commander of Pomeroon.

DE JONGHE, GEDEON MORRIS, settled on the Amazon before 1629, returned to Zealand in 1637. [HS.2nd series, vol.171]

DE KOLLOCK, SIMON, a Loyalist officer from Delaware who settled in Halifax, Nova Scotia, by 1786. [NA.AO13.21.268]

DE LAET, PAUL, a witness in Barbados, 1721. [BA: RB6/6/402]

DE LAET, SAMUEL, a witness in Barbados, 1721. [BA: RB6/6/445]

DE MART, JOHN, member of the crew of Captain Kidd's ship the <u>Adventure</u> 1696. [SPAWI.1700/354]

DEMETRIUS, CORNELIUS, on the Dutch Leeward Islands, 16...

DE MEY, PIETER, shipmaster in Curacoa, 1710.

DE MEYER, NICHOLAS, a Dutch inhabitant of New York, petitioned the Privy Council in 1668; 'a very old ill man' in New York, 1689. [SPAWI.1668.1885; 1689/667]

DE MEYER, WILLIAM, excise collector in Ulster County, New York, from 1693to 1699. [SPAWI.1698/978; 1699/231]

DE MILL, ISAAC, in New York, 1700. [SPAWI.1700/951]

DE MORG, CORNELIUS, a settler on Tobago before 1637. [HS.2nd series, vol.171/113]

DE NIENWERKERK, JACOB CLOOT, in Berbice, 1819. [NAS.RD5.167.185]

DE PESTER, JOHN, born in Holland, settled in New York as a merchant before 1674. [NA.HCA.De Pester V. The Bachelor, 1675]

DE PETERSON, JACOB, a merchant on Curacao, 1730s

DE PEYSTER, ABRAHAM, in New York, attorney for Benjamin de Jeune, 1686; in New York, 1691; was appointed Mayor of New York, 1698; Deputy Auditor of New York, 1704; Treasurer of New York, 1709; 1710. [SPAWI.1686.896; 1691/1771; 1692/1990; 1698/855; 1700/909; 1702/292; 1709/617, 802; 1710/517] [JCTP.Vol.I/251]

DE PEYSTER, ABRAHAM, jr., Treasurer of New York, 1722; 1724; 1726; 1727. [SPAWI.1724/191; 1726/379i; 1727/379][JCTP.Vol.Y/163]

DE PEYSTER, Major A. C., in Detroit, 5 April 1780; 29 December 1780; 29 August 1781. [HMC.A.II/109, 225, 325]

DE PEYSTER, A., Captain of the King's American Regiment, 24 June 1782. [HMC.A.II/535]

DE PEYSTER, CORNELIA, in New York, 1701. [SPAWI.1701/381]

DE PEYSTER, CORNELIUS, at Fort William Henry, New York, 1700. [SPAWI.1700/702]

DE PEYSTER, ISAAC, in New York, 1700. [SPAWI.1700/951]

DE PEYSTER, JAMES, Commissary for French prisoners in New York, 1782. [HMC.A.III/48, 84, 182]

DE PEYSTER, JOHANNES, a member of the General Assembly of New York, 1699, 1702. [SPAWI.1699/317; 1702/292, 999]

DE PEYSTER, PIERRE, son of Pierre de Peyster, Bedford Patent, New York, from Newark, New Jersey, a Loyalist,

in New York, 1782; to London in 1782.
[HMC.A.III/211][NA.AO12.14.240]

DE PUTER, CORNELIUS, in Barbados, probate 29 October
1667. [BA.RB6/15/560]

DE RIEMER, ISAAC, in New York, 1700; purchased land
east of Huntington, Nassau Island, Suffolk County, New
York, 1702. [SPAWI.1700/953; 1702/351, 364]

DE RIEMER, PIETER, administrator of the estate of
Elizabeth Graveratt, New York, 1688; sheriff of New
York, 1698-1699; in New York, 1700.
[SPAWI.1688/1625; 1698/855; 1700/575]

DE RIEMER, PIETER, a glazier in New York, 1701.
[SPAWI.1701/584]

DE ROODT, JAN, member of the crew of Captain Kidd's ship
the Adventure 1696. [SPAWI.1700/354]

DE RUE, BALTHAZAR, in Curacao 1677.
[PCCol.1679/1246]

DE RUYTER, MICHAEL, Admiral of the Dutch fleet at
Martinique, 1674. [SPAWI.1674/1334]

DE SALVE, JAN MARIUS, Lieutenant Colonel, from Texel,
the Netherlands, on 6 November 1763 bound for
Berbice.

DE STALPERT, JACOB, Commander of St Eustatius from
1719 to 1720.

DE VALK, BAREND, master of the Avonturier at Surinam,
1787. [NWIC]

DE VEER, JOHAN, Governor of Curacao, 1783

DE VOS, CHRISTOFFEL, surgeon at Fort Kijkoveral,
Essequibo, 1701. [SPAWI.1701/624]

DE VOS, JAN, master of the <u>Prinses Royaal</u> at Surinam, 1775. [NWIC]

DE VOS, MATTHEUS, a merchant in the New Netherlands and by 1655 a soldier there. [GAA.NA.1029/211]

DE VRIES, DAVID, born 1593, from Hoorn, a navigator and adventurer, patroon in Surinam and on Staten Island. [HS.2nd series, vol.171]

DE WANDALAER, JOHANNES, a resident of Albany, New York, in 1700. [SPAWI.1700/845]

DE WEND, EDWARD MICHAEL, a Brevet Major of the 60th Regiment, died in St Anne's, Barbados, on 9 May 1816. [St Michael's Cathedral gravestone]

DE WETT, GARTON, from Delaware River, Ulster County, New York, a Loyalist soldier who settled in Montreal by 1783. [NA.AO12.33.219]

DE WIJS, ..., master of the Orphans Court in Berbice, 1763.

DE WINDT, JAN, sr., a settler on Saba .....[NWIC#619/18]

DE WINDT, JAN, born 1717, son of Jan de Windt, Commander of St Eustatius, died in January 1775.

DE WINDT, ..., Major of the Orange Rangers, Halifax, Nova Scotia, 1778, 1779. [HMC.A.I/361, 394, 417]

DE WINT, JOHN, in St Thomas, 1783. [HMC.A.IV/63]

DE WIT, ANN, widow of a farmer from Bloomingdale, a refugee in New York, 1782. [HMC.A.III/302]

DE WIT, CORNELIUS, was buried on 28 April 1674 in St Michael's graveyard, Barbados. [St Michael's burial register]

DE WIT, JAN, was naturalised in New York during 1728. [SPAWI.1729/1068]

DE WITT, DERRICK CLAES, deposition re Ulster County, New York, 1695. [SPAWI.1699/292]

DE WITT, GEORGE, a planter in Antigua, 1710. [SPAWI.1710/674]

DE WITT, PHILLIP, a planter in Nevis, 1712. [JCTP.Vol.P/224]; a hostage in Martinique, escaped in 1714. [SPAWI.1720/204]

DE WITT, THOMAS, a planter in Antigua, 1709. [SPAWI.1709/487]

DE WOLF, SABRA, on Long Island, New York, 1777. [See NA.AO13.25.262]

DECKER, PETER, in New Jersey, 1754. [JCTP.Vol.61/2/91]

DEN BOGERT, MINDERT, in Dutchess County, New York, dead by 1766. [see NA.AO12.25.222]

DEUSSUM, SAMUEL, master of the Vrienden at Surinam, 1790. [NWIC]

DIRICK, PHILIP, of Caldwell's Manor, New York, 1786. [NA.AO12.26.153]

DIRICKSEN, DOW, a shipmaster at Barbados, 1655. [SPAWI.1655/1973]

DITMARS, DOUWE, jr., from Queen's County, Long Island, New York, a Loyalist army officer who settled in St John, New Brunswick, by 1786. [NA.AO12.110.157]

DONCKER, JAN SIMONSZ., sr. on the Dutch Leeward Islands, 1689, Commander there from 1704 to his death in 1717.

DOUW, ANDRES, a resident of Albany, New York, in 1702. [SPAWI.1702/999]

DOUW, HENDRICK, a resident of Albany, New York, in 1700, 1702. [SPAWI.1700/845; 1702/999]

DROCK, JOHANNES, a member of the General Assembly of New York, 1699. [SPAWI.1699/317]

DU FAIJ, ..., Governor of Curacao, 1720s

DUYKINCK, G., in New York, 1690. [SPAWI.1690/1126]

DIRECKSEN, NYEC REALS, in Richmond County, New York, 1702. [SPAWI.1702/999]

DYCKMAN, CORNELIUS, formerly a farmer in Bergen County, then a refugee in New York, with his wife and two children also with three sons in the King's service, petitioned Governor Robertson on 24 January 1781; a witness in New York, 1786. [HMC.A.II/239]

DYKEMAN, GARRET, formerly of Westchester County, New York, settled in Queen's County, New Brunswick, in 1783. [NA.AO13.22.73]

EARHART, SIMEON, from Saratoga, Albany County, New York, a Loyalist soldier who settled on Isle aux Noix, Quebec, by 1786. [NA.AO13.81.84]

EBBING, JERONYMUS, a Dutch inhabitant of New York, petitioned the Privy Council in 1668. [SPAWI.1668.1885]

ECKERSON, JACOB, from New Hempstead, Haverstraw Precinct, Orange County, New York, a Loyalist soldier who settled on the Tusket River, Nova Scotia, by 1786. [NA.AO13.25.158]

ECKERSON, JOHN, from New Hempstead, Haverstraw Precinct, Orange County, New York, a Loyalist soldier who settled in Shelburne, Nova Scotia, by 1786. [NA.AO13.25.162]

ECKHOUT, ALBERT, born around 1610, an artist from 1637 to 1644 in the service of Count Maurice of Nassau, the Governor General of Dutch Brazil, later settled in Groningen and died in 1665.

EGBERSE, DERICK, a resident of Albany, New York, in 1702.[SPAWI.1702/999]

EGBERT, ABRAHAM, in Staten Island, New York, 1777. [NA.AO13.98.112]

EGBERT, ANTHONY, in Staten Island, New York, 1777, a Loyalist soldier who settled at St John, New Brunswick, by 1786. [NA.AO13.21.160]

EGBERT, TENNIS, in Richmond County, New York, 1702. [SPAWI.1702/364]

EGBERT, TUNIS, in Staten Island, New York, 1777. [NA.AO13.98.111]

ELBERTSEN, AERT, a boatman in New York, 1700. [SPAWI.1700/839]

ELLERBECK, EMANUEL, a carpenter in Poughkeepsie, Dutchess County, New York, pre 1783. [NA.AO12.32.205]

ELLIS, GARRET, in New York, 1776. [NA.AO13.98.117]

ELLIS, JAN, a planter at Savonet, Curacao, 1719

ELLIS, JAN, born in St Eustatius, settled in Willemstad, Curacao, in 1751 as a Dutch Reformed Church minister until 1771.

ELLIS, SEBASTIAN, in Staten Island, New York, 1776. [NA.AO13.98.118]

ELSEWORDT, GEORGE, in New York, 1700. [SPAWI.1700/951]

ENNISON, JACOB, a resident of Albany, New York, in 1702. [SPAWI.1702/999]

ESDRE, GODRIED C., settled on Curacao in 1731.

EVERSON, CORNELIUS, at New York in 1673. [SPAWI.1673.1143]

EVERTSE, HENRY, member of the crew of Captain Kidd's ship the Adventure 1696. [SPAWI.1700/354]

EVERTSE, JOHN, purchased land east of Huntington, Nassau Island, Suffolk County, New York, 1702. [SPAWI.1702/364]

EVERTSEN, Captain NICOLAAS, a resident of the New Netherlands, master of the Rammekens arrived in Essequibo via Surinam and Barbados in 1700. [SPAWI.1700/715]

EVERTSEN, ..., a Dutchman, to settle Providence Island, 1635. [SPCol.1574-1660:200]

FAESCH, ISAAC, Governor of the Dutch Leeward Islands fron 1737 to 1740, then Governor of Curacao from 1740 to 1758. [NWIC#585/49]

FALCONBROUGH, ISAAC, a resident of Albany, New York, in 1702.[SPAWI.1702/999]

FEYNESE, GERRET, a resident of Albany, New York, in 1702.[SPAWI.1702/999]

FICK, PETER, from Dover, Dutchess County, New York, settled in Maugerville, New Brunswick, by 1786. [NA.AO13.21.168]

FLIPS, HERMAN, a resident of Albany, New York, in 1702.[SPAWI.1702/999]

FLIPSE, FLIP, a resident of Albany, New York, in 1702. [SPAWI.1702/999]

FLIPSEN, FREDERICK, a councillor of New York, 1685, 1689, 1702. [SPAWI.1685.185; 1689/665; 1702/1206]

FLORISEN, NICHOLAAS, a shipmaster at Barbados, 1655. [SPAWI.1655/1973]

FOCK, BARTLETT, a shipmaster at Barbados, 1655. [SPAWI.1655/1973]

FORT, JACOB, in Half Moon District, Albany County, New York, 1786. [see NA.AO13.15.547]

FORT, JAN, a resident of Albany, New York, in 1702.[SPAWI.1702/999]

FRANC, CORNELIUS, a Dutch pirate on the La Paix 1700. [SPAWI.1700/523]

FREDRICKSE, MEINERT, a resident of Albany, New York, in 1702.[SPAWI.1702/999]

FREEHOUDT, ISAAC, of Saratoga, New York, pre 1782. [NA.AO13.12.514]

FRELICK, BENJAMIN, from Albany County, New York, a Loyalist soldier from 1778 to 1783, then settled at Niagara. [NA.AO12.28.38]

FROMAN, HENDRICK, a resident of Albany, New York, in 1702.[SPAWI.1702/999]

GALE, JAN, probably from Frisia, Governor of Curacao, 1738 to 1740. [NWIC.580/36, 229; 582/610; 583/229]

GARRET, JOHN, in Fresh Kill, Richmond County, New York, 1702. [SPAWI.1702/364]

GARRETSE, REIER, a resident of Albany, New York, in 1702.[SPAWI.1702/999]

GARRISE, JAN, a resident of Albany, New York, in 1702.[SPAWI.1702/999]

GARRITSON, SECKER, in Fresh Kill, Richmond County, New York, 1702. [SPAWI.1702/364]

GELSKERKE, HERMAN, secretary and in 1729 Commander of Essequibo until his death in 1742. [SPAWI.1718/777]

GERRITSE, ADRIAAN, alderman of New York, 1687. [SPAWI.1687/1424]

GERRITSE, ELBERT, a resident of Albany, New York, in 1700. [SPAWI.1700/845]

GERRITSE, HENDRICK, a fusilier who was wounded at La Prairie, 1691. [SPAWI.1691/1907, 1969, 2556]

GERRITSE, LUCAS, a resident of Albany, New York, in 1700, 1702. [SPAWI.1700/845; 1702/999]

GERRITSE, MARTE, in Albany, New York, 1687; was appointed a justice of the peace for Albany on 27 May 1691. [SPAWI.1687/1427;1691/1533]

GERRITSE, NICOLAS, in New York, 1691. [SPAWI.1691/1434]

GERRITSON, GERRIT, a Commissary at Albany, New York, 1666. [SPAWI.1666.1304]

GERRITSON, REYER, a resident of Albany, New York, in 1700. [SPAWI.1700/845]

GEYSELAR, ERY, member of the crew of Captain Kidd's ship the Adventure 1696. [SPAWI.1700/354]

GILLE, JAN, a Walloon laborer, with his wife and three children, to emigrate to Virginia 1621. (?). [SPCol.1574-1660:498]

GILLESEN, ..., a planter on the Peereboom plantation on the Berbice River, 1763.

GLEN, JOHANNES SANDERSE, witness to a contract made with the Mohawk Indians at Schenectady, New York, 26 December 1700; a resident of Albany, New York, in 1702 [SPAWI.1700/909; 1701/38; 1702/999]

GOTCHY, HANS, a shipmaster at Barbados, 1655. [SPAWI.1655/1973]

GOTHOUT, HENDRICK, a resident of Albany, New York, in 1700. [SPAWI.1700/845]

GOUT, FOB OUT, residing on the Delaware River, 1664. [SPAWI.1664.808]

GOUVERNEUR, ABRAHAM, was pardoned by the Privy Council, Colonial, on 7 April 1692. [PCCol.1680-1720.204]

GRAEFF, PIETER, an indentured servant in Barbados, 1645. [GAA.NA#1620]

GRAVENRAEDT, ANDRIES, in New York, 1701. [SPAWI.1701/871]

GREVERAET, ANDRIES, in New York, 1689. [SPAWI.1689/671]

GROENENDYCK, JOHANNES, a resident of Albany, New York, in 1700; collector of quit-rents in Albany, 1702. [SPAWI.1700/845; 1702/351]

GROSBAK, STEPHANUS, a resident of Albany, New York, in 1700; Commissioner of Indian Affairs of New York, at Albany in 1730. [SPAWI.1700/845; 1730/622]

GROSEBECK, JOHN, a merchant in Albany, New York, 1725. [SPAWI.1725/600][JCTP.Vol.BB/109]

GRUNWALD, ISAAC, a Dutch Reformed Church pastor on St Thomas, Danish West Indies, from 1716. [RAK.WIC.430]

GUALTIER, NICHOLAS, a Dutch prisoner in Jamaica, 1712. [SPAWI.1712/267]

HAISELLENHOIG, JOHANNES, in New York, 1687. [SPAWI.1687.1250]

HANSE, HENDRICK, Mayor of Albany, New York, 1699; 1700; a member of the House of Representatives of New York, 1701, 1720. [SPAWI.1699/250; 1700/909; 1701/1117; 1720/230]

HANSEN, HANS, in Barbados, probate 3 September 1656 Barbados. [BA.RB6/13/162]

HANSEN, MATHIAS, late of Ulster County, New York, dead by 1700. [SPAWI.1700/703]

HANSINCH, HENRICK, a resident of Albany, New York, in 1700. [SPAWI.1700/845]

HARDENBROOCK, BERNARD, a resident of New York, 1702. [SPAWI.1702/1206]

HARDENBURGH, JOHANNES, in Albany County, New York. 1776. [see NA.AO12.25.222]

HARING, ABRAHAM, of Herringtown, Bergen County, New Jersey, in London by 1784. [NA.AO13.96.390]

HARING, JACOB, a witness in New York, 1786. [NA.AO88/555]

HARINGMAN, MAARTEN, master of the St Maartensdijk, from the Netherlands to Berbice in 1763.

HARKEMER, JOOST, [Johan Joost Herchheimer], a farmer from Tryon County, New York, a Loyalist officer who settled at Cataraqua, New Brunswick, by 1786. [NA.AO12.26.139]

HARKENROTH, ..., secretary fiscal of Berbice, 1763

HARMAN, VALENTINE, from Claverack, Albany County, New York, a Loyalist soldier who settled in Quebec by 1786. [NA.AO13.81.148]

HARMENSEN, ALBERT, a resident of Albany, New York, in 1702.[SPAWI.1702/999]

HARMENSEN, FREDRICK, a resident of Albany, New York, in 1702.[SPAWI.1702/999]

HARMENSON, JOHANNES, a resident of Albany, New York, in 1700, 1702. [SPAWI.1700/845; 1702/999]

HARMENSON, TOMAS, a resident of Albany, New York, in 1700, 1702. [SPAWI.1700/845; 1702/999]

HARMESEN, NANNING, an Indian trader at Albany, New York, in 1686. [SPAWI.1687.1428]

HARMYSSE, FREDRICK, a resident of Albany, New York, in 1700. [SPAWI.1700.845]

HARPERDINCK, JOHANNES, a resident of New York, 1702. [SPAWI.1702/1206]

HARS, JACOB, a shipmaster and in 1676 Commander of Essequibo.

HART, JACOB, from English Neighborhood, New Jersey, Loyalist refugees bound for Nova Scotia, 1783. [HMC.A.IV/195]

HARTMAN, DAVID, from Tomhanick, Albany County, New York, a Loyalist soldier who settled in Sorel, Nova Scotia, by 1784. [NA.AO12.28.225]

HARTMAN, ELIZABETH, in St Kitts, 1712. [JCTP.Vol.P/243]

HARTMAN, JOAN, in Nevis, 1712. [JCTP.Vol.P/245]

HARTSEN, BARNARDUS, an Indian trader in the Sinnekes country, New York, 1730. [SPAWI.1730/622]

HARTSHORN, LAWRENCE, of New York city, 1784. [NA.AO12.110.95]

HASSEL, PIETER, a planter on St Maarten, around 1730

HATTINGA, ..., an army captain in Berbice, 1763.

HAULENBECK, ISAAC, paymaster of the New Jersey Volunteers, New York, 1782, 1783. [HMC.A.III/146, 166, 197, 329]

HEELEN, HENDRIK J., master of the Drie Gezusters at Surinam, 1758. [NWIC]

HEGEMAN, DENIS, in King's County, Nassau Island, New York, 1702. [SPAWI.1702/999]

HEINSIUS, JOHANNES, Governor of Surinam, 1678

HEISE, VAN BENT, a resident of Albany, New York, in 1702.[SPAWI.1702/999]

HENDRICK, ..., a Dutch skipper of a New York sloop, 1699. [SPAWI.1699/680]

HENDRICKS, HENDRICK, a constable in Ulster County, New York, 1695. [SPAWI.1699/292]

HENDRICKSEN, JACOB, a shipmaster at Barbados, 1655. [SPAWI.1655/1973]

HENDRICKSEN, LEONARD, a planter in Nevis, 1712. [JCTP.Vol.P/224]

HENDRICKSON, ISAAC, in New York, 1776. [NA.AO12.110.67]

HENDRICKSON, STEPHEN, in Queen's County, Long Island, New York, 1776. [NA.AO12.110.81]

HENDRICKSZOON, JAN, settled on the River Wiapoco before 1625. [HS.2nd series, vol.171/270]

HENLEN, HEN., Commissioner for Indian Affairs, at Albany, New York, 1711. [SPAWI.1711/863]

HENLYNE, ANDRIES, from Curacao to New York in 1699. [SPAWI.1699/680]

HENNEKYNE, JOHN, in Port Royal, Jamaica, probate July 1693 Jamaica.

HENRICHSEN, HENRICH, a Dutch Reformed Church minister on St Croix, Danish West Indies, 1742. [RAK.WIC.429]

HERMANS, CASPAR, in Bohemia, Maryland, 1689, 1690. [SPAWI.1689/632; 1690/1164]

HERRING, ABRAHAM, of Tappan, New Jersey, 1782. [NA.AO13.80.187]

HERRING, CORNELIUS, in English Neighborhood, New Jersey, 1783. [HMC.A.IV/73, 74]

HERRING, DERICK, of Bergen, New Jersey, 1783. [NA.AO12.110.15]

HERRING, PIETER, a member of the House of Representatives of New York, 1701. [SPAWI.1701/1117]

HESSEN, JAN, in Tobago or Nevis, 1678. [SPAWI.1678/849]

HESSEN, WILLEM, a lawyer who settled in Curacao in 1783. [NWIC]

HEYLIGER, JOHAN, Commander of St Eustatius, from 1730 to 1736, Governor of Berbice from 1764. [NWIC][SPAWI.1737/318]

HODIJEMANS, ANDRIES, a member of the House of Representatives of New York, 1701. [SPAWI.1701/1117]

HOFMAN, JOHAN LAMBERT URBAN BARCEL, a Dutch Reformed Church minister on St Croix, Danish West Indies, 1757. [RAK.WIC.429]

HOGELANT, HENDRICK, in New Jersey, 1749. [PCCol.1750/485]

HOGOBOME, DERICK, a resident of Albany, New York, in 1702.[SPAWI.1702/999]

HOLLANDER, ADRIAAN, Councillor of Essequibo, to Barbados, 1700. [SPAWI.1700/429]

HOOF, PIETER CORNELIUS, indicted and tried on a charge of piracy, in Boston, New England, on 18 October 1717 and found guilty. [SPAWI.1718/575]

HOOGLANDT, ADRIEN, in New York, a prisoner in 1702, discharged on 16 April 1703; a merchant in New York, 1712. [SPAWI.1702/1166, 1199; 1702-03/585; 1712/433]

HOOGLANDT, DYRK JANSEN, in New York, 1700. [SPAWI.1700/817]

HOPPER, CONRAD, a tenant farmer in Tryon County, New York, before 1776, father of Abraham Hopper, settle in Williamsburg, Quebec, by 1788. [NA.AO13.81.154]

HORST, ENGELBERT, a military engineer and inspector of fortification of Curacao, 1767

HOSSEN, JOHN, in Tobago, 1678. [PCCol.1678/1237]

HOUSEMAN, ABRAHAM, naturalised in New York, 1735. [SPAWI.XLI.591]

HOWLETT, NATHANIEL, a merchant from Amsterdam, probate 20 January 1653 Barbados. [BA.RB6/11/546]

HUBER, ZACHARIAS, naturalised in New York, 1735. [SPAWI.XLI.591]

HUDDE, ANDRIES, secretary of the New Netherlands from 1632 to 1638, treasurer in 1635. [GAA.NA#318/64] [ARA.OWIC.Inv.50/32]

HUYGEN, LEENDERT, a prisoner in New York, 1702. [SPAWI.1702/1166]

JACOBS, CLAUS, a resident of Albany, New York, in 1702.[SPAWI.1702/999]

JACOBSEN, HARPERT, a mariner in Jamaica, 1688; a resident of Albany in 1702. [SPAWI.1702/999; 1735/181]

JACOBSEN, HEN., in New York, 1702. [SPAWI.1702/999]

JACOBSEN, WILLIAM, a resident of Albany, New York, in 1702.[SPAWI.1702/999]

JACOBSON, CORNELIUS, a pirate who was imprisoned in Jamaica during 1665. [SPAWI.1665.950]

JANSE, ANDRES, a resident of Albany, New York, in 1702.[SPAWI.1702/999]

JANSE, JOSEPH, a resident of Albany, New York, in 1700. [SPAWI.1700/845]

JANSE, LAMBER, a resident of Albany, New York, in 1702.[SPAWI.1702/999]

JANSE, PETER, a poor man in Fresh Kill, Richmond County, New York, 1702. [SPAWEI.1702/337]

JANSEN, ANDRIES, member of the crew of Captain Kidd's ship the Adventure 1696. [SPAWI.1700/354]

JANSEN, GARRET, a shipmaster at Barbados, 1655. [SPAWI.1655/1973]

JANSEN, JOHANNES, in New York, 1724. [SPAWI.1724/409]

JANSEN, JOHN, a Dutch inhabitant of New York, petitioned the Privy Council in 1668. [SPAWI.1668.1885]

JANSEN, STOFFELL, a Dutch inhabitant of New York, petitioned the Privy Council in 1668. [SPAWI.1668.1885]

JANSZOON, GERRIT, a merchant, to the New Netherlands aboard the St Jacob, master Haye Janszoon, in 1646. [GAA.NA#734B/80]

JANSZOON, KLAAS, a merchant, to the New Netherlands aboard the St Jacob, master Haye Janszoon, in 1646. [GAA.NA#734B/80]

JANTE, ANDRIES, a resident of Albany, New York, in 1700. [SPAWI.1700/845]

JOCHEMS, MARRITGE, was contracted, in Amsterdam to work as a servant for five years in the New Netherlands by Anna Hendricks wife of Jacob de Hinse the surgeon at Fort Orange, in 1657. [GAA.NA#1206/159]

JOOST, JAN, was granted land in New York, 1686. [SPAWI.1686/952]

KALS, JOANNES G., a minister of the Dutch Reformed Church in Surinam from 1731 to 1733.

KARSTENSEN, WARNAER, a resident of Albany, New York, in 1700. [SPAWI.1700/845]

KERFBYL, CATHERINA, a widow in New York, deposition dated 10 November 1714. [SPAWI.1735/181]

KERSTEADE, CORNELIUS, a resident of New York, 1702. [SPAWI.1702/1206]

KERSTEADE, JACOB, a resident of New York, 1702. [SPAWI.1702/1206]

KERSTEADE, LUYCAS, son of the deceased Sarah Rooletts, in New York, 1702. [SPAWI.1702/20]

KEIFT, WILLEM, late Dutch governor of the New Netherlands, 1700. [SPAWI.1700/703]

KEMBALL, JORIS, to serve under the militia captain for Newtown, New York, 1691. [SPAWI.1691/1865]

KERCKRINCK, WILLEM, Governor of Curacao 1686 to 1692. [NWIC#468/103]

KETEL, DAVID, a resident of Albany, New York, in 1702. [SPAWI.1702/999]

KETEL, WILLIAM, a resident of Albany, New York, in 1702. [SPAWI.1702/999]

KETTNER, CHRISTIAAN, master of the Jonge Joachim at Surinam, 1772.[NWIC]

KIDIRE, JOHN, a resident of Albany, New York, in 1700. [SPAWI.1700/845]

KIERSTED, JACOBUS, in New York, 1731, co-owner and master of the sloop Two Brothers of New York which, when bound from Pennsylvania to South Carolina, was captured off Carolina by the Spanish on 22 August 1727. [SPAWI.1727/807iia;1731/94]

KIERSTED, JESSE, in New York, 1731, co-owner of the sloop Two Brothers which was captured off Carolina by the Spanish on 22 August 1727. [SPAWI.1731/94]

KIP, ABRAHAM, a resident of Albany, New York, in 1700. [SPAWI.1700/845]

KIP, JAMES, from Westchester, New York, a Loyalist soldier who died in Cumberland County, Nova Scotia, around 1783. [NA.AO12.26.235]

KIP, SAMUEL, son of Benjamin Kip from North Castle, Westchester County, New York, a Loyalist officer who settled in Cumberland County, Nova Scotia, by 1786. [NA.AO12.23.196]

KIP, ZIPHARAH, son of James Kip from Westchester, New York, settled in Halifax, Nova Scotia, by 1786. [see NA.AO12.26.235]

KIPP, JOHANNES, an Alderman of New York, 1691, a resident of New York, 1702; son in law of the deceased Sarah Rooletts, in New York, 1702; 1724. [SPAWI.1691/1370; 1702/20, 1206; 1724/409]

KIPP, THOMAS, from North Castle, Westchester County, New York, a Loyalist soldier who settled in Annapolis County, Nova Scotia, by 1786. [NA.AO.13.24.299]

KNEVEL, JOHANN WERMER, a Dutch Reformed Church minister on St Jan, Danish West Indies, 1752. [RAK.WIC.429]

KOCHERTHAL, CHRISTIAN, in New York, 1724. [SPAWI.1724/392v]

KOCK, WILLEM, a merchant and planter on Curacao, 1750. [NWIC#598/869]

KOCK, WILLEM, master of the Katy at Surinam, 1790. [NWIC]

KOLYER, JACOBUS, of Freshwater Pond, New York, 1780. [NA.AO12.110.125]

KOOL, PIETER JANSZOON, a merchant, to the New Netherlands aboard the St Jacob, master Haye Janszoon, in 1646. [GAA.NA#734B/80]

KORTWRIGHT, LAWRENCE, a merchant in New York city, 1778. [NA.AO12.75.175]

KOUVENHOVEN, GERRIT, in New York city, 1776. [NA.AO13.97.551]

KREISLER, JOHANNES, from Tryon County, New York, moved to New Johnstown, Canada, by 1786. [NA.AO12.32.171]

KRETTS, HENRICK, a trumpeter, emigrated via Leith, Scotland, aboard the St Andrew on 14 July 1698 bound for Darien, Panama. [NAS.CC8.8.83]

KRETTS, PAUL, a trumpeter, emigrated via Leith, Scotland, aboard the St Andrew on 14 July 1698 bound for Darien, Panama. [NAS.CC8.8.83]

KRUSE, CORNELIUS, in Richmond County, New York, in 1777. [NA.AO13.97.552]

KRUSE, HENRY, in Richmond County, New York, in 1777. [NA.AO13.97.553]

KUCH, PHILIP, from Richmond County, New York, a Loyalist soldier who died on 14 September, 1778, father of Peter Kuch who settled in Halifax, Nova Scotia. [NA.AO13.24.250]

KUYPER, JAM CORLELISSEN, a shipmaster, from Essequibo to Middelburg, Zealand, in 1700. [SPAWI.1700/715]

LAKERMAN, ABRAHAM, in Richmond County, New York, 1702; an Assemblyman of New York, 1708. [SPAWI.1702/364; 1708/157]

LAMONT, ISAAC, Commander of Bonaire, Secretary to the Raad of Curacao, Commander of St Eustatius, 1700 to 1704.

LANSINCK, GERRET, a burgher of Albany, New York, 1666. [SPAWI.1666.1219]

LECA, JAN, a Walloon laborer, with his wife and five children, to emigrate to Virginia 1621. (?). [SPCol.1574-1660:498]

LEECKER, FREDERICK, in St Kitts, petitioned for denization in 1662. [SPAWI.1662.269]

LEFFERT, HARMAN, at Oyster Bay, Long Island, New York, 1776. [NA.AO12.110.55]

LEGER, JAN, master of the West Cappelle at Surinam, 1776. [NWIC]

LEMMERS, ABRAHAM, an army lieutenant in Surinam, 1730

LEMMEX, H. E., a witness in Essequibo, 1802. [NAS.RD3.298.262]

LENT, ADOLPH, from Orange County, New York, husband of Clasie ..., parents of Abraham, James, Peter (dead by 1783), Maria wife of Guysbert Bogart, and Elizabeth wife of Cornelius Mabee. Adolph, a Loyalist refugee in New York city died on 8 October 1780. [NA.AO12.109.194]

LENT, PETER, from Orange County, New York, a Loyalist, dead by 1782, husband of Maria... [NA.AO13.40.96]

LEONARDSZOON, JAN, a shipmaster at Barbados, 1655. [SPAWI.1655/1973]

LEWIS, BARENT, in Poughkeepsie, New York, 1760. [see NA.AO12.25.222]

LICHTENBERG, PHILIP JULIUS, Governor of Surinam, 1670. [SPAWI.1670/219]

LINDERBECK, PHILIP, from Dutchess County, New York, a Loyalist soldier, to settle in New Brunswick, 1789. [NA.AO13.137.443]

LINDESAY, JOHAN, on the Dutch Leeward Islands, late Governor of St Eustatia, escaped to St Kitt's in April 1729. [SPAWI.1729/684]

LINDESAY, MARGARITTA, born on St Eustatius, married Luca de Wint on St Thomas, Danish West Indies, 1740. [RAK.WIC.429]

LINSING, HENDRICK, a resident of Albany, New York, in 1702.[SPAWI.1702/999]

LOCKERMANS, JACOB, a resident of Albany, New York, in 1702.[SPAWI.1702/999; 1702-03/748]

LODEWYCX, PIETER, and his son Jan Pieterse Lodewycx, from Flushing, settled on the Wiapoco River, returned to the Hague in 1615. [HS.2nd series, Vol.171/158]

LODOWYCK, CHARLES, in New York, 1689. [SPAWI.1689/667]

LOET, CORNELIS, master of the Waterguis at Surinam, 1781.[NWIC]

LONCQ, HENDRICK CORNELISZOON, arrived at Pernambuco in February 1630.

LOOCKERMAN, GOUERT, in Maryland, 1713. [SPAWI.1713/503]

LOOMAN, ANTHONY DIRCKSEN, in Essequibo, 1700. [SPAWI.1700/715]

LOOMAN, BERNARD, a member of the crew of Captain William Kidd's ship Adventure, 1700. [SPAWI.1700/354]

LOOTEN, OOK VAN DIRCK, a clerk, to the New Netherlands in 1659.

LORESE, CLAUSE, a resident of Albany, New York, in 1702.[SPAWI.1702/999]

LORNE, PETER, a cooper from Zealand, husband of Margaret Robertson, emigrated from Leith, Scotland, to Darien, Panama, aboard the Unicorn on 14 July 1698. [NAS.CC8.8.83]

LOTT, ABRAHAM, in New York city, husband of Cornelia Rapalje, 1745. [see NA.AO12.22.295]

LOUCKS, ABRAHAM, in Kinderhook, Albany County, New York, pre 1783. [NA.AO12.31.402]

LOUCKS, GEORGE, of Turlock, Tryon County, New York, 1786. [NA.AO12.29.289]

LOUCKS, JACOB, a farmer at Kinderhook, Albany County, New York, pre 1776, father of Jacob, both died at Oswego. [NA.AO112.64.282]

LOUCKS, WILLIAM, in Kinderhook, Albany County, New York, around 1783. [NA.AO13.80.265]

LUCAS, CLAUS, a resident of Albany, New York, in 1702.[SPAWI.1702/999]

LUCASON, GERRET, a resident of Albany, New York, in 1702.[SPAWI.1702/999]

LUERSE, CARSTEN, mariner in New York, trading with Captain William Kidd, 1699. [SPAWI.1699/669, 740]

LUKES, JACOB, from Kinderhook, Albany County, New York, a Loyalist who settled at the Bay of Quinte by 1788. [NA.AO12.31.396]

LULS, GERARD, the Slave Trade Commissioner at Willemstad, Curacao, 1700. [NWIC#200/43]

LUTTEN, H. C., a witness in New Amsterdam, Berbice, 1819. [NAS.RD5.167.185]

LUYKASSEN, GARRIT, journeyed to the Indians at Onnondage, 1700. [SPAWI.1700/702]

LUYKASSEN, JOHANNES, a resident of Albany, New York, in 1700. [SPAWI.1700/845]

LUYSTER, CORNELIUS, born 1719, a Loyalist who was imprisoned in Boston, Poughkeepsie, and in the prison ship at Esopus, petitioned Sir Henry Clinton in 11 October 1779. [HMC.A.II/49]

LYDEKKER, Reverend GERRIT, a minister of the Dutch Reformed Church in English Neighborhood, Bergen County, New Jersey, before 1776, a Loyalist in New York, 1782, in London 1784. [HMC.A.III/268-269] [NA.AO12.14.9]

MAAS, WILHELMUS, a book-keeper and secretary of the Dutch West India Company at Fort Kyck, Overal, Rio Essequibo, dead by 1700. [SPAWI.1700.429, 715]

MABIE, PETER, from Tryon County, New York, a Loyalist soldier who settled at Niagara by 1786. [NA.AO12.28.82]

MAERSCHALK, AND., an Alderman of New York, 1723; 1727. [SPAWI.1723/606; 1727/763v]

MAERTMAN, PIETER JANSZOON, a Dutch pirate or privateer in the Caribbean during 1630s. [HS.2nd series, vol.171/419]

MAGNUS, CARL, master of the Hoop at Surinam, 1779. [NWIC]

MARCELIS, GYSBERT, a resident of Albany, New York, in 1700. [SPAWI.1700/845]

MARIUS, PIETER JACOB, in New York, 1683, 1689, 1702. [SPAWI.1683.1372; 1689/188; 1702/1206]

MARSELIS, AHASUERUS, a resident of Albany, New York, in 1700, 1702. [SPAWI.1700/845; 1702/999]

MARSELIS, GISBERT, a resident of Albany, New York, in 1702.[SPAWI.1702/999]

MARTENS, JOHN, a Dutch inhabitant of New York, petitioned the Privy Council in 1668. [SPAWI.1668.1885]

MARTENS, POWLES, a resident of Albany, New York, in 1702.[SPAWI.1702/999]

MATHIJS, CLARA, contracted, in Amsterdam on 28 April 1639, as an indentured servant for five years in New Amsterdam. [GAA.NA#1555A/591]

MAURICIUS, JAN JACOB, born 1692, Governor of Surinam from 1742, died in Hamburg in 1768.

MAURITZ, JACOB, born in Harlem, Holland, in 1645, settled in New York in 1659, a mariner. [NA.HCA.Rex v.The Anne and Katherine, 1692]; a pilot in New York, 1702. [SPAWI.1702/20]

MAURITZ, JACOB, a memorial re events in New York between 1690 and 1691, dated Amsterdam, 15 October 1691. [SPAWI.1691.1840]

MEBE, PETER, a resident of Albany, New York, in 1702.[SPAWI.1702/999]

MEGAPOLENSIS, Reverend JOHN, in the New Netherlands, 1664. [SPAWI.1664.788]

MEGAPOLENSIS, SAMUEL, in the New Netherlands, 1664. [SPAWI.1664.788]

MEINDERSTE, FREDRICK, a resident of Albany, New York, in 1702.[SPAWI.1702/999]

MEINDERSTE, JOHANNES, a resident of Albany, New York, in 1702.[SPAWI.1702/999]

MEINDERSTE, REINER, a resident of Albany, New York, in 1702.[SPAWI.1702/999]

MELOTT, JOHN PETERSE, blacksmith in New York, 1700. [SPAWI.1700/951]

MEYER, ANDRIES, in New York, 1689. [SPAWI.1689/459]

MEYER, JAN FREDERICK, an army captain in Surinam, 1757

MEYER, JOHN, in New York, 1689. [SPAWI.1689/459]

MEYERS, MARTINUS, Commander of St Maarten, 1711.

MICHEELS, JOHN, in Fresh Kill, Richmond County, New York, 1702. [SPAWI.1702/364]

MILLER, JOHANN GEORGE, from Leeuwarden, a
Lutheran preacher who settled in Curacao in 1757.

MINGUEL, DIRECK, a resident of Albany, New York, in
1700. [SPAWI.1700/845]

MINGUEL, JER., in New York, 1702. [SPAWI.1702/999]

MINGUEL, JOHANNES, a resident of Albany, New York, in
1700, 1702. [SPAWI.1700/845; 1702/999]

MINTHORNE, PHILLIP, an Alderman of New York, 1727.
[SPAWI.1727/763v]

MOELAERT, GIJSBRECHT, master of the <u>Verwagting</u> at
Surinam, 1791. [NWIC]

MOESE, WILLIAM, a resident of New York, 1702.
[SPAWI.1702/1206]

MONTANACQ, JOHANN ARNOLD, a Dutch Reformed
Church minister, husband of Elisabeth Barner, on St
Thomas, Danish West Indies, 1753. [RAK.WIC.429]

MUTRUN, JACOB, a member of the House of
Representatives of New York, 1701.
[SPAWI.1701/1117]

MYNDERSE, REYER, a resident of Albany, New York, in
1700. [SPAWI.1700/845]

MYNDERSEN, BURGER, a blacksmith at Fort William
Henry, New York, in 1702. [SPAWI.1702/387]

NAP, CLAES, master of the <u>Jonge Jacob</u> at Surinam, 1775.
[NWIC]

NEPVEU, JAN, from Amsterdam, Governor of Surinam,
1770s. [NWIC]

NOELS, ANDRIES, master of the <u>Laurenburg</u> at Paramaribo,
1773. [NWIC]

NOORSTRANDT, JACOB, a nailer supplying Fort William Henry, New York, in 1702. [SPAWI.1702/387]

NORDHOEK, JOHANNES, master of the Jonge Willem at Paramaribo, 1773. [NWIC]

NOTELMAN, COENRAET, secretary of the New Netherlands, 1634. [ARA.OWIC.Inv.50/32]

OBELE, JOHN, a resident of Albany, New York, in 1702.[SPAWI.1702/999]

OESTERMAN, THOMAS, in Antigua, 1709. [SPAWI.1709/443]

ONDERDONCK, ADRIAEN, of Hampstead, Long Island, New York, 1778. [NA.AO12.110.39]

OOISCHOTT, ABRAHAM, a cabinet-maker in Port Royal, Jamaica, probate 22 March 1683 Jamaica.

OOISCHOTT, JAMES, a tailor in Port Royal, Jamaica, 1683.[see Abraham Ooischott's will]

OORBAN, WILLEM, master of the Jonge Samuel at Surinam, 1772.[NWIC]

OOTHOUT, HENDRICK, a resident of Albany, New York, in 1702.[SPAWI.1702/999]

OOTHOUT, JOHANNES, a resident of Albany, New York, in 1700, 1702. [SPAWI.1700/845; 1702/999]

ORVYN, CORNELIUS, member of the crew of Captain Kidd's ship the Adventure 1696. [SPAWI.1700/354]

OUDEN, NICOLAES, from the Netherlands on the Black Eagle, settled on the River Wiapoco in May 1625, Governor. [HS.2nd series, vol.171]

OYSTERMAN, JOHN, a planter in Nevis, 1712. [JCTP.Vol.P/224]

PAPE, JACOBUS, of the Dutch West India Company at Fort Kyck, Overal, Rio Essequibo, 1700. [SPAWI.1700.715]

PARMYTER, PAROCULUS, in New York, 1699. [SPAWI.1699/740]

PEAKE, JACOBUS, a resident of Albany, New York, in 1702.[SPAWI.1702/999]

PEECK, JACOBUS, from Harrington, New Jersey, in New York, 29 November 1779, settled in Granville, Nova Scotia, by 1786. [HMC.A.II/68][NA.AO13.80.386]

PEECK, SAMUEL, a farmer in Bergen County, New Jersey, before 1776, a militia captain, in New York, 29 November 1779, settled in Granville, Nova Scotia, by 1786. [HMC.A.II/68][NA.AO13.26.348]

PEEK, DAVID, formerly of Schraalenburg, Bergen County, New Jersey, commander of a Loyalist Militia Volunteer Company in New York, 1779, deceased by 1786. [HMC.A.I/399, 414][NA.AO13.80.377]

PERSEL, DAVID, soldier of a Loyalist Militia Volunteer Company in New York, husband of Margaret, 1779. [HMC.A.I/399]

PETEROM, JAN, a shipmaster at Barbados, 1655. [SPAWI.1655/1973]

PETERS, JAMES, from Orange County, New York, a Loyalist who settled in St John, New Brunswick, by 1786. [NA.AO13.22.194]

PETERS, THOMAS, from Dutchess County, New York, a Loyalist who settled in Queen's County, New Brunswick, by 1786. [NA.AO12.25.103]

PHILLIPS, ADRIAN, Assemblyman of New York, 1708. [SPAWI.1708/157]

PHILLIPS, FREDRICK, an inhabitant of New York or Albany, petitioned the Privy Council, Colonial, to permit

his ship The Fort of Albany of New York, to sail from
Amsterdam to New York, in 1669. [PCCol.1669/842]

PHILLIPS, FREDRICK, in New York, 1700; Alderman of
New York, 1727; Judge of the Exchequer Court of New
York, 1733. [SPAWI.1700/951; 1727/763; 1733/324]

PHILLIPS, MARGARITA, a Dutch inhabitant of New York,
petitioned the Privy Council in 1668.
[SPAWI.1668.1885]

PHILLIPS, SAMUEL, a smith in New York, 1700.
[SPAWI.1700/951]

PHILLIPSE, ADOLPH, Councillor of New York, 1705;
Speaker of the House of Assembly of New York, 1729;
letters dated 21 December 1730 and 29 April 1736.
[SPAWI.1729/966; 1730/624; 1736/298][JCTP.Vol.K.4]

PIETERSE, CARL, master of the Maria at Surinam, 1775;
master of the Vrijheyt at Surinam, 1780. [NWIC]

PIETERSEN, ADAM, in Philadelphia, Pennsylvania, 1702.
[SPAWI.1702/270]

PIETERSZOON, ABRAHAM HEYLIGER, Vice
Commander of St Maarten from 1746.

PIETERSZOON, SYMON, a shipmaster at Barbados, 1655.
[SPAWI.1655/1973]

PIJPERSBERG, ENGELBERT, in Essequibo, 1760s.
[NWIC#1026/573]

PINHORNE, GURTRYDA, in Flushing, New York, 1782,
widow of Lieutenant Pinhorne who died before 1776.
[HMC.A.III/60]

POST, CHRISTIAAN, master of the Vrugt at Surinam, 1792.
[NWIC]

POST, FRANS, born in 1612, an artist in Brazil ca.1645 to
1665, died in 1680.

POST, GARRIT, of Staten Island, New York, 1777.
[NA.AO13.92.167]

POST, ISAAC, a Loyalist, from Orange County, New York,
1781, then a Loyalist refugee on Staten Island in 1782,
later, by 1786, in Shelburne, Nova Scotia.
[HMC.A.II/502][NA.AO13.25.406]

POST, PETER, of Staten Island, New York, 1776.
[NA.AO13.92.169]

POTMAN, VICTOR, a resident of Albany, New York, in
1702.[SPAWI.1702/999]

POULIS, SYMOEN, a clerk of the Dutch West India
Company at Fort Kyck, Overal, Rio Essequibo, 1700.
[SPAWI.1700.715]

PRAAL, ARENT, in Fresh Kill, Richmond County, New
York, 1702. [SPAWI.1702/364]

PROVOOST, D., a member of the General Assembly of New
York, 1699. [SPAWI.1699/317]

PROVOOST, JOHAN, a memorial re events in New York
between 1690 and 1691, dated Amsterdam, 15 October
1691. [SPAWI.1691.1840]

PRUS, PETER, in Johnstown, Tryon County, New York,
settled in Quebec by 1786. [NA.AO12.31.272]

PRUYN, JOHANNES, at Albany, New York, 1720.
[SPAWI.1720/230]

QUACKENBOS, ADRIAN, a resident of Albany, New York,
in 1700. [SPAWI.1700/845]

QUACKENBOS, WOUTER, a resident of Albany, New
York, in 1702.[SPAWI.1702/999]

QUAST, JOHANNIS, a Dutch Reformed Church minister in
Curacao from 1757

QUINTOR, HENDRICK, indicted and tried on a charge of piracy, in Boston, New England, on 18 October 1717 and found guilty. [SPAWI.1718/575]

RACER, GEORGE FRIDERICUS, a Dutch Reformed Church minister on St Croix, 1744. [RAK.WIC.429]

RAECX, EVERARD, in service of the New West India Company in Curacao and from 1728 the Commander or Governor of St Eustatius. [SPAWI.1729/684]

RAMRING, ..., a minister of the Dutch Reformed Church in Berbice around 1763.

RAPALJE, ABRAHAM, an innkeeper from Bushwick, Long Island, New York, died in 1781. [NA.AO13.16.170]

RAPALJE, DANIEL, a farmer from Newtown, Long Island, New York, settled in Nova Scotia by 1784. [NA.AO13.92.225]

RAPALJE, GEORGE, [Joris], a farmer from Newtown, Long Island, New York, with his wife Dina, and children John, Gerrit, Cornelia and Antje, settled in Nova Scotia by 1784. [NA.AO13.92.225; AO12.22.295]

RAPALJE, JOHN, from Brooklyn, Long Island, a Loyalist in 1776, possibly son of George or Joris Rapalje, in London by 1784. [NA.AO12.73.219]

RAPALJE, THOMAS, in Charlotte Precinct, Dutchess County, New York, 1786. [NA.AO13.16.66]

RASVELT, WIGBOLDUS, a Dutch Reformed Church minister on St Thomas, Danish West Indies, from 1728; in Curacao from 1730 until his death in 1757. [RAK.WIC#430][NWIC#588/646]

RATEERE, JACOB, from Curacao to New York in 1699. [SPAWI.1699/680]

REINIES, EDWARD, a resident of Albany, New York, in 1702. [SPAWI.1702/999]

REINING, JAN ERASMUS, a privateer and master of the De Koning Balthazar in the West Indies around 1690.

RENZLAER, RICHARD, a Commissary at Albany, New York, 1666. [SPAWI.1666.1304]

RESEVELT, NICHOLAS, in New York, 1702. [SPAWI.1702/1092]

REYNDERS, BARENT, in New York, 1702. [SPAWI.1702/1092]

RICKMAN, ALBERT, a resident of Albany, New York, in 1702.[SPAWI.1702/999]

RICKMAN, ALBERT, jr., a resident of Albany, New York, in 1702.[SPAWI.1702/999]

RICKMAN, HARMAN, a resident of Albany, New York, in 1702.[SPAWI.1702/999]

RIDNER, CONRAD, a Loyalist, formerly of Bergen County, New Jersey, by 1787 in Fredericton, New Brunswick. [NA.AO88/556]

RIESE, LODEWIJK, master of the Cornelia at Surinam, 1790. [NWIC]

RIETVELD, DIRK, master of the Gulden Vrijheyt at Surinam, 1775, and the Zeenymph at Surinam, 1793. [NWIC]

RIEUWERTSZOON, WILLEM, a councillor of the New Netherlands in 1636. [ARA.OWIC.Inv.51/28]

RINK, WILLEM HENDRIK, a lawyer who settled in Demerara in 1781, later Vice-Commander of St Maarten from 1790 to 1807.

RISCH, JACOB, a resident of Albany, New York, in 1700. [SPAWI.1700/845]

RITZEMA, RUDOLPHUS, a lawyer and interpreter in New York city pre 1776, a Loyalist. [NA.AO12.101.46]

ROELOFSSE, THE., in New York, 1689. [SPAWI.1689/217]

ROELOOFS, PIETER, an indentured servant in Barbados, 1645. [GAA.NA#1620]

ROL, HENDRIK, Commander of Essequibo, from 1670 until his death on 31 March 1676.

ROLDAN, MARTIN, a Roman Catholic priest on Curacao, 1747.

ROMBOUGH, JACOB, from Tryon County, New York, settled in Montreal by 1786. [NA.AO12.31.314]

ROOS, GERRIJT, in New York, 1692. [SPAWI.1692/2678]

ROOS, PAUL F., a planter and poet in Surinam, 1786.

ROOSEBOOM, Captain , an Indian trader at Albany, New York, 1686. [SPAWI.1687/1428]

ROOSEBOOM, HENDRICK, journeyed to the Indians at Onnondage, 1700. [SPAWI.1700/702]

ROOSEBOOM, JOHANNES, a resident of Albany, New York, in 1700. [SPAWI.1700/845]

ROOSEBOOM, Captain JOHANNES, at Albany, New York, 1711. [SPAWI.1711/863]

ROOSEBOOM, JOS., in New York, 1702. [SPAWI.1702/999]

ROOSEVELT, JOHN, an Alderman of New York, 1727. [SPAWI.1727/763v]

ROOSIBOOM, GERRETT, a resident of Albany, New York, in 1700. [SPAWI.1700/845]

ROSEE, JAN, a resident of Albany, New York, in 1702.[SPAWI.1702/999]

ROSENS, DANIEL, in Tobago or Nevis, 1678. [SPAWI.1678/849][PCCol.1678/1237]

RUDOLPHUS, SERVAS, master of the Epiminondas at Surinam, 1785. [NWIC]

RUITER, JOHN, from Hoosick, Albany County, New York, a Loyalist officer who settled in St John, New Brunswick, by 1786. [NA.AO12.26.171]

RUNNELS, JOHN, born on St Eustatius, a preacher there.

RUTGERS, ANTHONY, in New York, 1723; petitioned for the swamp, New York, granted 12 August 1731. [SPAWI.1723/606] [JCTP.Vol.HH/79/114/124/239]

RUTGERS, ANTHONY, a merchant in New York city, 1783. [NA.AO12.111.55]

RUTSON, JACOB, in Ulster County, New York, 1698; a member of the General Assembly of New York, 1699; 1702. [SPAWI.1698/593i; 1699/317; 1702/1206]

RYCKEMAN, JOHN, in New York, 29 November 1779. [HMC.A.II/68]

RYCKMAN, ALBERT, a resident of Albany, New York, in 1700. [SPAWI.1700/845]

RYCKMAN, JOHN, from Tappan, Orange County, New York, father of Tobias etc, moved to Sorel, Canada, in 1783, died by 1786. [NA.AO12.29.354]

RYCKMAN, Mr......, in New York, 1782. [HMC.A.III/362]

RYDER, CHRISTOPHER, in New York, 1776. [NA.AO12.111.33]

RYERSEN, GERRIT, was appointed a justice of the peace in Albany, New York, on 27 May 1691. [SPAWI.1691/1533]

RYKMAN, ALBERT, an alderman of New York, 1687. [SPAWI.1687/1424]

RYNDERS, JOHANNES, in Poughkeepsie, New York, around 1760. [see NA.AO12.25.222]

RYNDERSON, BARENT, in New York, 1700. [SPAWI.1700/951]

SAGE, JAN, a Walloon serge-maker, with his wife and four children, to emigrate to Virginia 1621. (?). [SPCol.1574-1660:498]

SALOMEE, DAVID, master of the Wulpenburg at Surinam, 1757. [NWIC]

SALOMONSZOON, JOHANNES, Commander of St Eustatius, 1696 to his death in 1690.

SANDERS, BARENT, Commissioner of Indian Affairs of New York, at Albany in 1730. [SPAWI.1730/622]

SANDERS, SALOMON, an overseer in Surinam, 1722. [NWIC#250/12]

SANDERSSE, ROBERT, a resident of Albany, New York, in 1700. [SPAWI.1700/845]

SAYCAR, GERRETT, a resident of Albany, New York, in 1700. [SPAWI.1700/845]

SCHAAK, JOHN, Captain of the 57th Regiment, imprisoned near Chatham, letter 1782. [HMC.A.III/224]

SCHABEL, MICHAEL ALEXIUS, a Jesuit in Curacao around 1715.

SCHEE, HERMANUS, was naturalised in Maryland in 1702. [SPAWI.1702/242]

SCHELLINX, CORNELIUS, deposition, 1699.
[SPAWI.1699/343]

SCHENCK, ABRAHAM, from Newton, Queen's County,
Long Island, New York, 1784. [NA.AO13.367]

SCHENCK, JOHANNES, was appointed schoolmaster at
Flatbush, New York, 1691. [SPAWI.1691/1785]

SCHENCK, JOHN, of Cow Neck, Long Island, New York,
1783. [NA.AO12.110.89]

SCHENCK, MARTIN, of Cow Neck, Long Island, New
York, 1783. [NA.AO12.110.89]

SCHENCKNIGH, BERNARD, a merchant in Barbados,
1676. [PCCol.1676/1102]

SCHERMERHOORN, JACOB, a Dutch inhabitant of New
York, petitioned the Privy Council in 1668.
[SPAWI.1668.1885]

SCHERMERHOORN, RYER, from Albany, New York, to
the Maquaase in May 1699; a member of the House of
Representatives of New York, 1701, 1702.
[SPAWI.1699/740; 1701/1117; 1702/337, 1007]

SCHERMERHOORN, WILLIAM, a farmer from
Helderberg, Albany County, New York, a Loyalist
soldier who settled in Canada, his wife Elizabeth was at
the Bay of Quinte in 1784. [NA.AO12.28.198]

SCHERNICHEORN, BEYERS, a member of the General
Assembly of New York, 1699. [SPAWI.1699/317]

SCHEURMAN, or MARROW, ISABEL, on Montserrat,
1699. [SPAWI.1699/132, 683]

SCHEURMAN, JACOB, passenger on the Scottish ship at
New York, 1699. [SPAWI.1699/718]

SCHEURMAN, PETER, a tailor on Antigua, 1709.
[SPAWI.1709/459]

SCHICK, CHRISTIAN, a blacksmith in Tryon County, New
York, then a soldier of the King's Royal Regiment of
New York, settled in Johnstown, Nova Scotia, by 1786.
[NA.AO12.29.366]

SCHIEFFELIN, JACOB, from Detroit, a Loyalist soldier
from 1777 to 1784, settled in Montreal by 1785.
[NA.AO13.81.358]

SCHIRMEISTER, ..., a member of the Council of Berbice,
1763.

SCHMIT, ERIK, a shipmaster at Barbados, 1655.
[SPAWI.1655/1973]

SCHOHANHOVA, HENDRICK, a resident of Albany, New
York, in 1702.[SPAWI.1702/999]

SCHOHANHOVA, JACOBUS, a resident of Albany, New
York, in 1702.[SPAWI.1702/999]

SCHORER, LUCAS, Commander of the Dutch garrison at
Fort Orange, St Eustatius, 1689.

SCHUT, ALEXANDER, from Dutchess County, New York,
settled in Half Moon District, Albany County, New
York, before 1776, moved to Canada in 1780.
[NA.AO12.26.405]

SCHUYDACKER, CHRISTIAN, to serve under the militia
captain for Flatbush, New York, 1691.
[SPAWI.1691/1865]

SCHUYLER, ABRAHAM, in New York, 1691; a resident of
Albany, New York, in 1700, 1702. [SPAWI.1691/1611;
1700/845; 1703/999]

SCHUYLER, ARENT, brought Shawnee Indians from
Philadelphia to New York in 1692. [SPAWI.1692/2678]

SCHUYLER, BRANDT in New York, 1689, 1702.
[SPAWI.1689/667; 1702/999, 1206]

SCHUYLER, DAVID, from New York to Canada in 1698; a
resident of Albany in 1700, 1702. [SPAWI.1698/822;
1700/845; 1702/999]

SCHUYLER, DIRCK, a merchant in New York, 1725.
[SPAWI.1725/600]

SCHUYLER, JACOBUS, a resident of Albany, New York, in
1700, 1702. [SPAWI.1700/845; 1702/999]

SCHUYLER, JOHANNES, Justice of Albany, New York,
suspended, 1699, 1702; Commissioner of Indian Affairs,
1711, 1730. [SPAWI.1699/740; 1702/999; 1711/863;
1730/622]

SCHUYLER, Captain JOHN, a messenger to the Indians in
New York, 1699. [SPAWI.1699/245]

SCHUYLER, JOHN, in New Jersey, 1738. [PCCol.1720-
1745.833]

SCHUYLER, JOHN CORTLANDT, of Bethlehem, Albany
County, North America, probate August 1797 PCC

SCHUYLER, MYNDERT, a resident of Albany, New York,
in 1700; possibly a tradesman at Fort William Henry,
New York, in 1702; 1703; 1718; was appointed as
Mayor of Albany in 1720; Commissioner for Indian
Affairs, 1711, 1720, 1730.
[SPAWI.1700/845; 1702/387, 999; 1702-03/748;
1711/863; 1720/48; 1723/230; 1730/622]
[JCTP.Vol.T/440]

SCHUYLER, NICHOLAS, at Albany, New York, in 1711.
[SPAWI.1711/863]

SCHUYLER, OLIVER, in New York, 1723.
[SPAWI.1723/606]

SCHUYLER, PETER, resigned his share of Mohawk lands on 19 April 1698; a resident of Albany, New York, petitioned the Privy Council, Colonial, for reimbursement arising from his costs among the Five Nations and resisting the French, 20 April 1710; President of the Council of New York, 1720. [PCCol.1680-1720/621; 1707/182] [JCTP.Vol.W/233]

SCHUYLER, Colonel PETER, of New Jersey, died on 24 January 1762. [GM: 32.194]

SCHUYLER, PETER, Senator for western New York, died in Montgomery County on 4 January 1792. [GM:62.182]

SCHUYLER, PHILIP PIETER, a Commissary at Albany, New York, 1666; Mayor of New York, 1687; Mayor of Albany, 1689, 1703; Commissioner for Indian Affairs, 1709. [SPAWI.1666.1304; 1687/1424; 1689/667; 1702-03/29, 100, 822, 1078; 1709/196]

SCHUYLER, Lieutenant PHILIP, died in New York 1725.[SPAWI.1725/655]

SCHUYLER, Major General PHILIP, in Philadelphia, Pennsylvania, letters, 1777; 1791-1796. [HMC.A.I/87, 89, 112][NLS.ms3310]

SCHUYLER, PHILLIP, a resident of Albany, New York, in 1700, 1702. [SPAWI.1700/845; 1702/999]

SCHUYLER, PIETER, a military officer at Albany, New York, in 1691; a resident of Albany, in 1702. [SPAWI.1691/1968; 1702/999]

SCHUYLER, PIETER, President of the Council of New York, 1719. [SPAWI.1719/488 etc]

SCHWARTZ, SIMON, a blacksmith in Conajoharie, Tryon County, New York, a Loyalist soldier before 1783. [NA.AO12.28.233]

SCHYLER, BRANDT, in New York, 1751. [JCTP.Vol.60/32]; Mayor of New York, died in 1752. [GM:22.478]

SEAGARDT, FEILYST, a widow in Bergen Neck, New Jersey, 1783. [NA.AO13.87.93]

SEBRING, CORNELIS, a member of the General Assembly of New York, 1699, 1701, 1708. [SPAWI.1699/317; 1701/1117; 1708/157]

SELS, JOOST, Rear Admiral, died in Curacao in September 1759.

SEROOSKERKE, POULUS, an employee of the Dutch West India Company at Fort Kyck, Overal, Rio Essequibo, before 1700. [SPAWI.1700.715]

SEY, JOHANNES, a councillor of New York, 1685. [SPAWI.1685/186]

SHAAF, JOHN THOMAS, from Maryland, a medical student at Edinburgh University from 1788 to 1790, died in 1817. [EUL]

SIERENS, JAN DE LATOMBE MATTHYS, in Essequibo, 1700. [SPAWI.1700/715]

SIJBRANTSSON, TORSTEN, an indentured servant in Barbados, 1645. [GAA.NA#1620]

SIJMENSZOON, MICHIEL, councillor of the New Netherlands in 1635. [ARA.OWIC.Inv.50/32]

SISNET, CORNELIUS, a planter in Barbados, probate 27 March 1662 Barbados. [BA.RB6/15/174]

SLICKTONHORST, GERRITT, a Dutch inhabitant of New York, petitioned the Privy Council in 1668. [SPAWI.1668.1885][PCCol.1668/819]

SLINGERLANDT, ALBERT, a resident of Albany, New York, in 1702.[SPAWI.1702/999]

SMITH, PETER, "a Dutchman" on St Thomas, 1699.
[SPAWI.1699/616]

SONNEMANS, PIETER, son of Arent Sonnemans who died
in Scotland, from Rotterdam, emigrated via Scotland to
East New Jersey in 1685 (?), land grant there in 1686;
petitioned the King in 1699; Councillor of New Jersey,
1708; 1709; 1711, 1720; petitioned the Privy Council,
Colonial, 6 July 1716.
[EJD.LiberA/287][SPAWI.1699/164, 205; 1709/819 etc;
1711/835; 1717/112] [JCTP.Vols.M/169; W/333]
[PCCol.1680-1720.474, 709, 819]

SPATER, JOHANES, naturalised in New York, 1735.
[SPAWI.XLI.591]

SPEGHT, PHILIP, a Dutch Reformed minister on Curacao
from 1668 to 1679.

SPITSENBERGH, THEUNIS CORNELIS, a Commissary at
Albany, New York, 1666. [SPAWI.1666.1304]

SPONS, JAN, member of the crew of Captain Kidd's ship the
Adventure 1696. [SPAWI.1700/354]

STAATS, BAARENT, in Albany, New York, 1703.
[SPAWI.1702-03/620]

STAATS, JACOB, a surgeon at Albany, New York, 1699.
[SPAWI.1699/215]

STAATS, JOACHIM, in New York, 1701.
[SPAWI.1701/584]

STAATS, SAMUEL, in New York, 1689; deposition, 1699;
petitioned the Council of New York in 1702; deceased
by 1716. [SPAWI.1689/780; 1699/878; 1702/292]
[JCTP.Vol.R/380]

STAETS, Captain ABRAHAM, a Commissary at Albany,
New York, 1666. [SPAWI.1666.1304]

STAFFMAKER, DAVID, a memorial re events in New York between 1690 and 1691, dated Rotterdam, 16 October 1691. [SPAWI.1691.1842]

STAM, DIRCK CORSZOON, councillor of the New Netherlands in 1635. [ARA.OWIC.Inv.50/32]

STAP, PIETER, master of the Vlissingen at Surinam, 1758. [NWIC]

STEDMAN, JOHN GABRIEL, a soldier and author in Surinam, 17.... [NWIC#349][NAS.GD99.229.9/2]

STEENDAM, JACOB, to the New Netherlands in 1652 aboard the Hoff van Cleeff, master Adriaen Bloemmart. [GAA.NA#2279/III/73]

STEENWICK, CORNELIUS, in the New Netherlands, 1664. [SPAWI.1664.788]; in New York, 1683. [SPAWI.1683.1372]

STERNBERGEN, MATHEW, a Dutch inhabitant of New York, petitioned the Privy Council in 1668. [SPAWI.1668.1885]

STEVENS, JACOB, Commander of St Eustatius from 1721 to 1722.

STEVENSEN, JAN, from Dordrecht, an employee of the Dutch West India Company at Fort Kyck, Overal, Rio Essequibo, returned to the Netherlands aboard the Brandenburg in 1700. [SPAWI.1700.715]

STEVENSON, OLOFF, a resident of New York or Albany, then in Amsterdam, successfully petitioned King Charles II for permission to return to New York from Amsterdam aboard the Fort Albany of New York on 1669. [SPAWI.1669.29]

STOLL, JOOST, Ensign of Captain Leisler's company in New York, 1689. [SPAWI.1689/352]

STORM VAN 'S GRAVESANDE, LAURENS, born in 's Hertenbosch in 1704, a soldier, then in 1737 Secretary of Esequibo, and in 1742 Commander there until 1772, died in the colony on 14 August 1775. [NWIC#1026/52;1027/100]

STORM VAN 'S GRAVESANDE, JONATHAN SAMUEL, Commander of Demerara from 1752.

STORTSOFT, GARRET, in King's County, Nassau Island, New York, 1702. [SPAWI.1702/999]

STOUTENBERGH, PETER, in Bergen Neck, New Jersey, 1783. [NA.AO13.87.93]

STOUTENBURGH, ..., Captain of a company of soldiers in South Carolina, 1723. [JCTP.Vol.Z/104]

STOWE, JOHN, born 1613, from Flushing, Zealand, settled in Bermuda. [NA.HCA.Barkely v. Morris, 1669]

STRAET, DIRK, formerly of Haverstraw, Orange County, New York, but in New York by 1783. [see NA.AO13.16.145]

STRIDETHOLL, CONRAD, a merchant in Barbados, probate 30 May 1650 Barbados. [BA.RB6/13/124]

STRYCHER, GERARD, was appointed Sheriff of King's County, New York, 19 March 1691. [SPAWI.1691/1366]

STUYLING, WILLEM, a planter on Curacao, 1766. [OAC#900/18]

STUYVESANT, Gr., an Alderman of New York, 1727. [SPAWI.1727/763v]

STUYVESANT, N.W., an Alderman of New York, 1685. [SPAWI.1685.186]

STUYVESCANT, OLIVER, petitioned the Privy Council, Colonial, to trade between Amsterdam and New York in 1668. [PCCol.1668/819]

STUYVESCANT, PIETER, Governor of the New Netherlands, 1664. [SPAWI.1664.788]

SUELMAN, CORNELIS, in Surinam, 1676. [SPAWI.1676/943]

SVARTE, JACOB, a Dutch Reformed Church minister on St Thomas, Danish West Indies, 1731. [RAK.WIC#431]

SWAERTWOUT, THOMAS, in New York, 1702. [SPAWI.1702/1206]

SWALLENBERG,......, an Ensign in Surinam, 1730.

SWART, ENNIS, a resident of Albany, New York, in 1702.[SPAWI.1702/999]

SWART, JOSIAS, a resident of Albany, New York, in 1702.[SPAWI.1702/999]

SWART, SCHOUT, a Commissary at Albany, New York, 1666. [SPAWI.1666.1304]

SWITS, ISAAC, a resident of Albany, New York, in 1702.[SPAWI.1702/999]

SWITS, SYMON, a resident of Albany, New York, in 1702.[SPAWI.1702/999]

SYLVESTER, CONSTANT, in Barbados by 1654, [see BA.RB6/13/56]; probate 18 January 1671 Barbados, [BA.RB6/8/316]

SYMONSEN, PIETER, a shipmaster at Barbados, 1655. [SPAWI.1655/1973]

SYN, JAN, a resident of Albany, New York, in 1700. [SPAWI.1700/845]

TELLER, GASPAR, was appointed Sheriff of Albany County, New York, 19 March 1691. [SPAWI.1691/1366]

TELLER, JOHANNES, a resident of Albany, New York, in 1702.[SPAWI.1702/999]

TELLER, WILLIAM, son in law of the deceased Sarah Rooletts, in New York, 1702. [SPAWI.1702/20]

TEMMINCK, HENDRIK, Governor of Surinam, 1721 to 1727. [NWIC]

TEN BROECK, DIRCK, Commissioner of Indian Affairs of New York, at Albany in 1730. [SPAWI.1730/622]

TEN BROECK, WESSEL, Justice of Albany, New York was suspended in 1699; a resident of Albany in 1700, 1702, 1720. [SPAWI.1699/740; 1700/845; 1702/999; 1720/230]

TEN ECK, COENRAET, a prisoner in New York, 1702. [SPAWI.1702/1166]

TEN EYCK, KEENRAET, a resident of Albany, New York, in 1700. [SPAWI.1700/845]

TEN OEVER, THEODORUS, a Catholic priest on Curacao from 1759.

THIELEN, GERARD, an army lieutenant at Fort Nassau, Berbice, 1763.

THIRRY, JAMES, a merchant from Amsterdam, and his wife Mary Van Rijn, probate 19 July 1680 Barbados. [BA.RB6/10/201]

THISSO, ABEL, acting Governor of Surinam in 1677.

THOMAS, JOHN, a memorial re events in New York between 1690 and 1691, dated Amsterdam, 15 October 1691. [SPAWI.1691.1840]

TIENHOVEN, NICOLAS, a shipmaster from New York to Bristol in 1702. [SPAWI.1702/853]

TILLABACK, MARTINAS, from Stone Arabia, Tryon County, New York, a Loyalist soldier who settled in New Johnstown, Quebec, by 1786. [NA.AO13.81.406]

TIMMER, THOMAS, was naturalised in New York during 1728. [SPAWI.1729/1068]

TROTZ, GEORGE HENDRIK, a planter in Essequibo, Commander of Essequibo in 1767, and Member of the Court of Justice.

TUNESE, EGBERT, a resident of Albany, New York, in 1702. [SPAWI.1702/999]

TUNESE, GERRET, a resident of Albany, New York, in 1702.[SPAWI.1702/999]

TUNISON, CORNELIUS, Assemblyman for the Eastern Division of New Jersey in 1703. [SPAWI.1702-03/1249]

TURCK, JACOB, in Albany, New York, 1702. [SPAWI.1702/999]

TYHOFF, J. H. M., a witness in Essequibo, 1802. [NAS.RD3.298.262]

UPPRANCHARD, CORNELIUS RENARD, master of the Fortuyn van Amsterdam at Jamaica, 1668. [SPAWI.1668.1707]

USCHER, CHRISTIAAN GODLOBB, in Essequibo, 1700. [SPAWI.1700/715]

VAN AKEN, KOSTER, a Dutch inhabitant of New York, petitioned the Privy Council in 1668. [SPAWI.1668.1885]

VAN ALEN, WILLIAM, a resident of Albany, New York, in 1700. [SPAWI.1700/845]

VAN ALLEN, JACOB, from Tryon County, New York, a
Loyalist who settled in Quebec by 1786.
[NA.AO12.29.376]

VAN ALLEN, WILLIAM, from New Bridge, Hackensack,
Bergen County, New Jersey, a Loyalist officer in 1776,
later settled in Nova Scotia. [HMC.A.IV/195]
[NA.AO12.16.154]

VAN ALSTINE, ISAAC, of Susquehanna River,
Pennsylvania, a Loyalist soldier, settled at Coteau du Lac
by 1783. [NA.AO12.40.435]

VAN ALSTINE, JAMES, husband of Lydia ...., parents of
Lambert born 1765, Jonas born 1767, Isaac born 1773,
James born 1777, and Aaron born 1779, from the
Susquehanna River Patent, Pennsylvania. A Loyalist
soldier whose widow and children settled in Montreal by
1786. [NA.AO12.28.237]

VAN ALSTINE, LAMBERT, of Wioming, Pennsylvania,
father of Isaac Van Alstine in Fredericksburg, North
America, probate October 1790 PCC

VAN ALSTINE, PETER S., born in Kinderhook, Albany
County, New York, a gentleman and a Loyalist in New
York, 1777; a Loyalist militia officer; to New York on
the Mary in August 1778; settled in Montreal by 1783.
[HMC.A.I/268, 281][NA.AO12.33.91]

VAN ALSTYN, MATTHEW, at Fort George, New York, in
March 1736. [SPAWI.1736/267]

VAN AMBURGH, ABRAHAM, a Loyalist from Dutchess
County, New York, settled in St John, New Brunswick,
by 1786. [NA.AO13.21.430]

VAN AULA, WILLIAM, a resident of Albany, New York, in
1702.[SPAWI.1702/999]

VAN BAAL, JAN HENDRICKSE, in the province of New
York, 1775. [JCTP.Vol.82/108]

VAN **BALEN, JOHN,** a Dutch inhabitant of New York, petitioned the Privy Council in 1668. [SPAWI.1668.1885]

VAN **BATENBURG, ABRAHAM JACOB VAN IMBRYZE,** late Governor General of Berbice, died in Barbados on 9 October 1800. [St Michael's Barbados gravestone]

VAN **BATTENBURG, ...,** a planter in Berbice, dead by 1819. [NAS.RD5.167.185]

VAN **BEBBER, ISAAC,** was naturalised in Maryland in 1702. [SPAWI.1702/242]

VAN **BEBBER, MATTHIAS,** was naturalised in Maryland in 1702. [SPAWI.1702/242]

VAN **BECKE, Dr BALTHASAR,** factor for the Assiento at Curacao, 1684. [SPAWI.1684.1563]

VAN **BEEK, NICHOLAAS,** Governor of Curacao, 1701 to 1704. [NWIC.I/81; 200/70][SPAWI.1702-03/1327]

VAN **BELL, PIETER,** possibly on the island of New Tortola, or Tertholen in 1698; a planter and a free denizen of St Kitts petitioned King William in 1699; factor on St Thomas for the African Company of Emden, 1699; in May 1699 he sent 41 slaves to Nevis from St Thomas. which he claimed were for his family's use but were forfeited by the Admiralty Court in Nevis, petitioned the Privy Council in March 1704. [SPAWI.1698/156; 1699/648, 685][PCCol.1680-1720.459; 1704.119]

VAN **BELL, ...,** factor for the Assiento at Curacao, 1684; in St Kitts, 1704; probably from Amsterdam, an agent of the Brandenburg Company, in St Kitts, 1711; a planter in St Kitts, 1712, 1717. [SPAWI.1684/1563; 1711/391] [JCTP.Vols.I/88; K/31; P/230; T/22]

VAN **BERGEN, MARTEN GERRITSZOON,** councillor of the New Netherlands in 1635. [ARA.OWIC.Inv.50/32]

VAN BERGEYK, LAURENS LODEWIJK, Commander of Essequibo, from 1761 until his death in 1764.

VAN BEUNINGEN, JONATHAN, Governor of Curacao, from 1715. [RAC]

VAN BEVERHOUDT, LUCAS, a resident of the Dutch Leeward Islands in 1704.

VAN BERKEL, ADRIAAN, Secretary of Essequibo, 1670s, a plantation manager in Surinam from 1680-1689, author of *Travels in South America and Surinam.*

VAN BLARCOM, PETER, formerly in New Barbados, Hackensack, Bergen County, New Jersey, then by 1786 in Annapolis, Nova Scotia. [NA.AO13.26.504]

VAN BLARKUM, URIAH, probably from New Jersey, in Shelburne, Nova Scotia, by 1786. [NA.AO13.25.499]

VAN BLEAF, AARON, in Bergen County, New Jersey, prior to 1776. [see NA.AO12.15.340]

VAN BLOEMENDAAL, CLAES BORDINGH, a merchant, to the New Netherlands in 1647. [GAA.NA#1295/41]

VAN BOSVELDT, JACOB, Governor of Curacao, from 1761 to his death in July 1762. [NWIC#14/38]

VAN BRAAM, JACOB, was appointed as Major of the 60th Regiment on 8 July 1778, later in St Augustine, and in Savannah in July 1779. [HMC.A.I/122, 148, 277, 447, 480]

VAN BREEN, WILLEM, a memorial re events in New York between 1690 and 1691, dated Amsterdam, 15 October 1691. [SPAWI.1691.1840]

VAN BROUGH or VAN BRUGH, Captain PETER, at Albany, New York, 1700. 1711, and 1718. [JCTP.Vol.T/435] [SPAWI.1700/909; 1711/863;]

VAN BRUGH, Captain PHILIP, Commander of <u>HMS</u> <u>Chatham</u>, was appointed Governor of Newfoundland in April 1738. [JCTP.Vol.47/37]

VAN BRUGHEN or BRUGGE, JOHANNES, an alderman in New York, 1683, 1687. [SPAWI.1683.1106/1372; 1687/1250]

VAN BRUNT, CORNELIUS, a member of the General Assembly of New York, 1699, 1701, 1702, 1708. [SPAWI.1699/317; 1701/1117; 1702/29; 1708/157]

VAN BRUNT, HENDRICK, a member of the General Assembly of New York, 1699. [SPAWI.1699/317]

VAN BUREN, Dr JAMES, a surgeon from New Barbados, Hackensack, Bergen County, New Jersey, a Loyalist who settled in Granville, Nova Scotia, by 1784. [NA.AO.12.15.112]

VAN BURGH, JOHANNES, in New York, 1691. [SPAWI.1691/1750]

VAN BURKELOE, WILLIAM, in King's County, Nassau Island, New York, 1702. [SPAWI.1702/999]

VAN BUSKIRK, Dr ABRAHAM, from Bergen County, New Jersey, Lieutenant Colonel of the 3rd Battalion of the New Jersey Volunteers, a Loyalist officer who settled in Shelbourne, Nova Scotia, by 1788. [NA.AO.12.15.181] [HMC.A.IV/179, 376, 385, 427]

VAN BUSKIRK, DAVID, formerly in Kinnicameck, Bergen County, New Jersey, a Loyalist who moved to Richmond County, New York, by 1788. [NA.AO.13.100.386]

VAN BUSKIRK, JOHN, formerly of Morris County New Jersey, a Loyalist in 1776, later in Halifax, Nova Scotia. [NA.AO12.16.340]

VAN BUSKIRK, LAURENCE, a coroner's inquest on his body in New York, 19 May 1783. [HMC.A.IV/90]

VAN BUSKIRK, Captain LAWRENCE, son of John Van Buskirk, formerly a farmer in Hanover, Morris County, New Jersey, a Loyalist in New York, 16 March, 1779, 17 September 1779; settled in Halifax, Nova Scotia, by 1786. [HMC.A.I/399; II/35][NA.AO13.19.349]

VAN BUSKIRK, LAWRENCE, from Haversack Precinct, Orange County, New York, Captain of the King's Orange Rangers in 1777, father of Abraham, Thomas, etc, settled in Shelburne, Nova Scotia, by 1786. [NA.AO12.16.335]

VAN CAMP, JACOB, from Saratoga, Albany County, New York, settled in Quebec by 1786. [NA.AO12.29.289]

VAN CAMP, PETER, of Half Moon, Albany, New York, father of Jacob Van Camp at Matilda, North America, probate October 1790 PCC. [NA.AO12.29.292]

VAN CLEAF, BENJAMIN, sr., in Freehold, New Jersey, will dated 1747, father of John, Richard, and Benjamin, Elizabeth and Mary. [see NA.AO12.109.298]

VAN CLEAF, JOHN, son and executor of his father Richard Van Cleaf, New Jersey, around 1770. [see NA.AO12.73.103]

VAN CLEAF, RICHARD, in Freehold, New Jersey, will dated 1 September 1765, probate May 1776 Perth Amboy, husband of Elizabeth, father of Benjamin, John, Elizabeth, Hendiracha, Eleanor, and Mary. [see NA.AO13.9.397]

VAN CLECK, DANIEL, in New Jersey, 1783. [NA.AO12.110.11]

VAN CLEEFF, DIRCK, a resident of New York or Albany, then in Amsterdam, successfully petitioned King Charles II for permission to return to New York from Amsterdam aboard the <u>Fort Albany of New York</u> on 1669. [SPAWI.1669.29]

VAN COLLEN, JEREMIAS, Governor of Curacao, 1711 to 1715, died in January 1715.

VAN COLLEN, JUAN PEDRO, Commissioner of the Slave Trade and later Governor of Curacao, 1720s.

VAN CORTLANDT, FREDERICK, in New York, 1723. [SPAWI.1723/606]

VAN CORTLANDT, GERTRUDE, married Edward Buller, Captain of the Royal Navy, in Halifax, Nova Scotia, on 15 March 1789. [GM#59/371]

VAN CORTLANDT, JACOBUS, in New York, 1699, 1702, 1708, 1721. [SPAWI.1699/317; 1702/29, 248; 1708/157] [BA: RB6/6399]

VAN CORTLANDT, JOHANNES, in New York, 1689. [SPAWI.1689/667]

VAN CORTLANDT, OLAFFE STUYVESCANT, a Dutch inhabitant of New York, petitioned the Privy Council in 1668 for permission to trade between Amsterdam and New York. [SPAWI.1668.1885][PCCol.1668/819]

VAN CORTLANDT, O., a resident of New York, 1702. [SPAWI.1702/1206]

VAN CORTLANDT, PHILIP, formerly in Hanover, Morris County, New Jersey, then a Loyalist, Major of the 3rd Battalion, New Jersey Volunteers, John Street, New York, 1782, 1783, in London by 1783. [HMC.A.III/288, 336][NA.AO12.22.96]

VAN CORTLANDT, PHILLIP, councillor of New York, 1727; 1736; 1737. [SPAWI.1727/763; 1736/272; XLIII.190]

VAN CORTLANDT, STEPHEN, a councillor in New York, 1685, 1689, Commissioner and Receiver of the Revenue for New York in 1698. [SPAWI.1685.185; 1689/667] [SRO.Somers Papers]

VAN CORTLANDT, W., in New York, 1687.
[SPAWI.1687.1250]

VAN CORTLANDT, Miss, daughter of Major Van Cortlandt
in Halifax, Nova Scotia, married William Taylor from
London, in Cowley on 6 May 1791. [GM:61/488]

VAN COSTLAND, CATHERINE, daughter of Major Philip
van Costland in New York, married Dr William Gourlay,
a physician in Madeira, there on 25 April 1787.
[GM:57.637]

VAN CURLER, ARENT, a Commissary at Albany, New
York, 1666. [SPAWI.1666.1304]

VAN CURLER, JACOB, councillor of the New Netherlands
in 1635. [ARA.OWIC.Inv.50/32]

VAN CURLER, ONE, a resident of Albany, New York, in
1702.[SPAWI.1702/999]

VAN DAM, ANTHONY, an agent in New York, 1778.
[PCCol.1766-1783.458][NA.AO12.73.397]

VAN DAM, RIP, a merchant in New York, 1699, 1702, 1702,
1708, 1712; President of the Council of New York, 1732;
in Duchess County, New York, 1735; Councillor of New
York, 1735. [SPAWI.1699/317; 1702/1206; 1702-03/29,
100, 194; 1708/157; 1712/433; 1732/495; 1735/591;
1736/ misc;][JCTP.Vol. LL/141; 44/191]
[PCCol.1735/1046]

VAN DE CAR, RODOLPH, a tanner and shoemaker from
Cleverak, Albany County, New York, a Loyalist who
settled in Nova Scotia by 1783. [NA.AO12.33.153]

VAN DE LENDE, ROELOF, of Hackensack, New Jersey,
1783. [NA.AO12.110.91]

VAN DE VIER, PETER, in North Carolina, 1783.
[NA.AO12.111.5]

VAN DER BECK, ABRAHAM, formerly a farmer in
Harrington, Bergen County, a refugee in New York,
petitioned Governor James Robertson, 15 July 1781 and
10 December 1781, settled in Fredericton, New
Brunswick, by 1786. [HMC.A.II/300/362]
[NA.AO12.16.119]

VAN DER BECK, COENRAD, a resident of New York,
1702. [SPAWI.1702/1206]

VAN DER BECK, CORNELIUS, in New York, 1700.
[SPAWI.1700/140]

VAN DER BERGH, CORNELIUS, in New York, 15 January
1773. [PCCol.1766-1783.358]

VAN DER BERGH, FRANCIS, naturalised in New York,
1724. [SPAWI.1724/409]

VAN DER BERGH, JAMES, in Dutchess County, New York,
1780, 1783. [HMC.A.IV/99, 110]

VAN DE BERGH, VOLCKERT, in New York, 15 January
1773. [PCCol.1766-1783.358]

VAN DE BERGH, WILLIAM W., in New York, 15 January
1773. [PCCol.1766-1783.358]

VAN DER BOSCH, LAURENT, an Anglican minister in
Carolina and later in Boston, Massachusetts, 1685.
[SPAWI.1685.267]

VAN DER BURGH, DYRK, a bricklayer at Fort William
Henry, New York, 1698; petitioned the Council of New
York, 1701, 1702, 1703.[SPAWI.1700/575, 702, 845;
1701/126; 1702/187, 1206; 1702-03/680]

VAN DER BURGH, HENRICUS, in Pennsylvania, 1698; in
Newcastle, 1700 [SPAWI.1698/759; 1700/176]

VAN DER BURGH, HENRY, judge of the Inferior Court of
Dutchess County, New York, 20 August 1781, in New
York, 1783, a Loyalist who settled in St John, New

Brunswick, by 1786. [HMC.A.II/320; IV/387]
[NA.AO12.25.211]

VAN DER BURGH, NICHOLAS, formerly a farmer on
Cortland's Manor, New York, petitioned Governor
Tryon on 4 March 1780. [HMC.A. II/97]

VAN DER BURGH, PETER, from Dutchess County, New
York, a Loyalist who settled in St John, New Brunswick,
by 1786. [NA.AOO12.25.199]

VAN DER BURGH, RICHARD, from King's County, Long
Island, New York, son of judge Henry Van Der Bergh, a
Loyalist, husband of the widow of Abram Rapalje, in
London by 1784. [NA.AO12.25.60]

VAN DER BURGH, Captain, a planter on St Kitts, dead by
1714. [SPAWI.1714/630]

VAN DER DONCK, ADRIAEN, in Colendonck near New
Amsterdam, 1651. [GAA.NA#2279/24]

VAN DER DUSSEN, ALEXANDER, was granted 189 acres
in Granville County, South Carolina, on 18 January
1738. [NA.CO5/398]

VAN DER DUSSEN, Colonel, in South Carolina, 1752, 1754.
[JCTP.Vol.60/342; Vol.61/2/157]

VAN DER GOAST, ..., a shipmaster, bound from
Kirkcaldy, Scotland, to the West Indies on 7 September
1685. [NAS.E72.9.21]

VAN DER GRACHT, JAN CRYNSSEN, from Flushing to
Surinam on the Schakerloo in 1668. [SPAWI.1668.1746]
[PCCol.1668/769]

VAN DER GRIFT, PAUL LEENDERZEN, in the New
Netherlands, 1664. [SPAWI.1664.788]

VAN DER HAYDEN, MATTHIAS, member of the
Assembly of Maryland for Cecil County, 1701.
[SPAWI.1701/424]

VAN DER HEIGHDEN, DERICK, a resident of Albany, New York, in 1702.[SPAWI.1702/999]

VAN DER HEUL, HENDRICK, mariner in New York, trading with Captain William Kidd, 1699. [SPAWI.1699/669, 740]

VAN DER HEUVEL, JAN CORNELIS, Commander of Essequibo, from 1764 to 1767; 1778. [PCCol.1766-1783.516]

VAN DER HEYDEN, DYRICK, an Indian trader at Albany, New York, in 1686; a resident of Albany in 1700. [SPAWI.1687/1428; 1700/845]

VAN DER HEYDEN, MATHIAS, in Cecil County, Maryland, 1702; 1713. [SPAWI.1702/798; 1713/503]

VAN DER HEYDEN REESEN, PIETER, Secretary of Essequibo, 1707; 1708; 1710, 1711, 1718. [SPAWI.1708/281, 403, 600; 1710/214, 236, 257; 1711/779, 829; 1718/693, 778]

VAN DER HOESEN, HARME, in New York, 15 January 1773. [PCCol.1766-1783.358]

VAN DER HOOGE, JOOST, settled in Essequibo before 1616. [RAC#35]

VAN DER HORST, Miss, second daughter of Elias Van Der Horst, U.S.Consul, married John Duncombe Taylor, Captain of the 46th Regiment, in Antigua on 5 May 1798. [GM: 68.533]

VAN DER HOVEN, CORNELIUS, in New Jersey, ca1780. [NA.AO13.139.9]

VAN DER HYDE, PETER GAME, was granted 500 acres in Purrysburgh, South Carolina, on 10 April 1738. [NA.CO5/398]

VAN DER KELL, JAN JANSEN, a burgher of Albany, New York, 1666. [SPAWI.1666.1219]

VAN DER LINDE, JOHN, a merchant, died in Curacao on 4 January 1816. [GM:86.473]

VAN DER LIP, WILLIAM, a farmer from Northumberland County, Pennsylvania, a Loyalist soldier, settled at Niagara by 1787. [NA.AO12.40.422]

VAN DER NEARFE, WILLIAM, a witness in Barbados, 1703, probate 6 October 1703 Barbados

VAN DER NEARFEN, MARGARET, in St Peter's All Saints, Barbados, probate 25 August 1703 Barbados. [BA:RB6/10/557]

VAN DER PARRE, PIETER, master of the Vriendschap at Surinam, 1779. [NWIC]

VAN DER PLANK, JOHN, constable of Savannah, Georgia, dead by 20 December 1737. [SPAWI.XLIII.642]

VAN DER POEL. ISAAC, a refugee from Kinderhook, then in New York, petitioned Lieutenant General James Robertson on 4 July 1782, and Sir Guy Carleton on 22 January 1783. [HMC.A.III/7, 337]

VAN DER POOL, JAMES PILKINGTON, Councillor of St Kitts, 1775. [PCCol.1766-1783.573]

VAN DER POOL, JOHN, Councillor of Nevis, dead by 1775. [JCTP.Vol.82/59][PCCol.1766-1783.568]

VAN DER POOL, MALCOT, jr. a resident of Albany, New York, in 1702.[SPAWI.1702/999]

VAN DER POOL, MELGERT, a resident of Albany, New York, in 1700, 1702. [SPAWI.1700/845; 1702/999]

VAN DER POOL, THOMAS PILKINGTON, Councillor of St Kitts, 1775. [JCTP.Vol.82/78]

VAN DER SPIEGEL, JACOBUS, a prisoner in New York, 1702. [SPAWI.1702/1166, 1199]

VAN DER STERRE, DAVID, a physician in Curacao.

VAN DER STOOP, LEONARD, married Mary Mann, in St Michael's parish, Barbados, on 25 November 1687. [BA: PL1/1/367]

VAN DER VEEN, PAULUS, Governor of Surinam, 1696-1707.

VAN DER WARSUN, THOMAS, a witness in Barbados, 1712. [BA.RB6/7/74]

VAN DER WERF, BENJAMIN, late of Pennsylvania, 1706. [JCTP.Vol.L/10]

VAN DER WERF, FRANCIS, a witness in Barbados, 1681. [BA: RB6/14/227]

VAN DER WHERESTE, FRANCIS, wife Margaret, children William, Thomas, Anne, Francis, Elizabeth, and Nathaniel, St Peter's parish, Barbados, probate 7 September 1688 Barbados. [BA.RB6/41/69]

VAN DER WORFEN, ANN, married Joseph Gough, in St Philips, Barbados, on 28 July 1706. [BA:RL1/24/31]

VAN DER WORFEN, ELIZABETH, married William Jeffrys, in St Philips, Barbados, on 28 July 1706. [BA: RL1/24/18]

VAN DER WORTH, FRANCIS, father of William and Judith, in Barbados, 1668. [see J. Mossier's will, probate 6 April 1669 Barbados]

VAN DERSE, WOUTER, a resident of Albany, New York, in 1702.[SPAWI.1702/999]

VAN DICK, JACOBUS, a resident of Albany, New York, in 1702.[SPAWI.1702/999]

VAN DIJCK, HENDRICK, to the New Netherlands in 1645. [ARA.SG.LWI.Inv.5763.II]

VAN DIJCK, JAN, at Fort Kijkoveral, Essequibo, 1702. [SPAWI.1702/686]

VAN DINCKLAGEN, LUBBERT, treasurer of the New Netherlands in 1634; councillor of the New Netherlands in 1635. [GAA.NA.916/60][ARA.OWIC.Inv.50/32]

VAN DINE, DOUW, from Newtown, Long Island, New York, a Loyalist who settled in Canada by 1783. [NA.AO12.25.135]

VAN DOESBURCH, MARRITGE, a resident of New York or Albany, then in Amsterdam, successfully petitioned King Charles II for permission to return to New York from Amsterdam aboard the Fort Albany of New York in 1669. [SPAWI.1669.29]

VAN DORNE, JACOB, a rioter in Monmouth County, New Jersey, 1701. [SPAWI.1701/695]

VAN DOUTH, JAN, leader of a Dutch military force that arrived at Salvador da Bahia in May 1624.

VAN DUERSEN, JACOBUS, possibly a tradesman at Fort William Henry, New York, in 1702. [SPAWI.1702/387]

VAN DUSER, CONRAD, a farmer from Albany County, New York, a Loyalist who settled in Montreal by 1783. [NA.AO12.31.1]

VAN DYCK, HENDRICK, a surgeon at Albany, New York, 1699; a resident of Albany in 1700, in Richmond County, 1702. [SPAWI.1699/215; 1700/845; 1702/999]

VAN DYCK, HENRY, a candidate for holy orders in the Church of England, a refugee in New York, 27 September 1779. [HMC.A.II/41]

VAN DYCK, JACOBUS, a surgeon at Albany, New York, 1699; surgeon at the fort of Schenectady, New York, in 1701. [SPAWI.1699/215; 1701/584]

VAN DYKE, JOHN, from Somerset County, New Jersey, a Loyalist in 1776, later in London. [NA.AO12.13.127]

VAN DYKE, NICHOLAS, President, Newcastle, Delaware, 1783. [HMC.A.IV/37]

VAN DYNE, DOUW, late of Queen's County, North America, father of Cornelis Van Dyne, probate February 1789 PCC

VAN ELSLANDT, CLAES, councillor of the New Netherlands in 1635. [ARA.OWIC.Inv.50/32]

VAN EMBURGH, ADONIJAH, formerly in Bergen County, New Jersey, settled in Nova Scotia by 1786. [see NA.AO13.19.363]

VAN EMBURGH, JAMES, late of Barbados Neck, Bergen County, New Jersey, a Loyalist who settled on the Tusket River, near Shelburne, Nova Scotia, by 1786. [NA.AO12.16.1]

VAN EMBURGH, W. S., in Hackensack, New Jersey, 1774. [see NA.AO13.25.9]

VAN EMERSON, Mrs MARY, wife of Hartman Van Emerson in Barbados, 1664. [see BA.RB6/15/456]

VAN EPAN, EVERT, a resident of Albany, New York, in 1702. [SPAWI.1702/999]

VAN EPE, JAN BAPTIST, interpreter at Onnondage, New York, in 1699, interpreter at Albany, New York, in 1700; 1711. [SPAWI.1699/250; 1700/845; 1711/863]

VAN EPS, JAN BAPTIST, a resident of Albany, New York, in 1702.[SPAWI.1702/999]

VAN ERPECUM, JOAN, Governor of Curacoa, 1682 to 1685. [NWIC#832/347; 467/145][SPAWI.1683.1249]

VAN ESSEN, GEORGE, a Dutch Reformed Church minister on St Eustatius around 1740.

VAN ESTE, PETER, Assemblyman for the Eastern Division of New Jersey, 1703. [SPAWI.1702-03/1249]

VAN EVERY, MCGREGOR, a Loyalist from Albany County, New York, who settled in Niagara by 1783. [NA.AO12.32.218]

VAN FEURDEN, JANSEN, in New York, 1689. [SPAWI.1689/780]

VAN FLEEK, MARTE, a resident of Albany, New York, in 1702.[SPAWI.1702/999]

VAN GELDER, DANIEL, a burgher of Amsterdam, to the New Netherlands in 1635. [GAA.NA.944/463]

VAN GENT, HENRY, a witness in Barbados in 1698, [BA: RB6/16/149]; was naturalised in Barbados 1702. [SPAWI.1702/29, 336]

VAN GENT, MARIA, married Edward Maddox, in St Michael's, Barbados, on 30 October 1712. [BA:RL1/2/100]

VAN GIESIN, ABRAHAM, signed affidavits dated 18 November 1745 and 17 September 1747, New Jersey. [PCCol.1750.485]

VAN GILDER, Mrs, in Jamaica, 1699. [SPAWI.1699/443]

VAN GINNIS, LEENDART, a planter on the Rio Essequibo, before 1700. [SPAWI.1700.715]

VAN GORDEN, BENJAMIN, a soldier of the 2nd Battalion of the New Jersey Volunteers, who died coming from Philadelphia, certificate dated 25 February 1781, New York. [HMC.A.II/249]

VAN GORDEN, MARY, possibly from Katskill, widow of Benjamin Van Gorden of Colonel Morris's 2nd Battalion, New Jersey Volunteers, a refugee in New York who petitioned General Sir Henry Clinton on 18 February 1781, agreed to put her on the provision list on 1 May 1781. [HMC.A.II/247, 274]

VAN GOVEN, HENDRY, in New Providence, 1699. [SPAWI.1699/928]

VAN GROENEWEGEN, ADRIAAN, Commander of Essequibo, 1670s

VAN HAEGHEN, JAN, a resident of Albany, New York, in 1700. [SPAWI.1700/845]

VAN HANS, ABRAM, a merchant in New York, 1712. [SPAWI.1712/433]

VAN HECK, OLIVER, aged 35, his wife Katherin aged 34, and their son Peter aged 7, emigrated via London to Virginia on the Transport of London, master Edward Walker, in July 1635. [NA.E157/20]

VAN HESTON, SOPHIA, was transported from Leith, Scotland, to Maryland on 28 November 1704. [NAS.PC2.28.307]

VAN HEYTHUYSEN, GERARD, in New York, 1686, 1692. [SPAWI.1686.896; 1692/2129]

VAN HISE, JOHN, a refugee, possibly in New York, 22 November 1781. [HMC.A.II/353]

VAN HOOCK, LAURENCE, in New York, 1702. [SPAWI.1702/1206]

VAN HOOGENHEIM, SIMON, Governor of Berbice, 1763.

VAN HORN, ABRAHAM, Councillor in New York, 1722, 1735, 1736, 1737, Commissioner for settling the bounds between Rhode Island and Massachusetts Bay, 1738;

dead by 26 January 1744. [SPAWI.XLI.591;XLII.272; XLIII.190][JCTP.Vols. Y/225; 47/114; 52/12] [PCCol.1720-1745.833/834]

VAN HORN, CORNELIUS, Commissioner for settling the bounds between Rhode Island and Massachusetts Bay, 1738; resigned as councillor of New Jersey in 1745. [JCTP.Vols. 47/114; 53/81]

VAN HORN, LAURENCE, a miller from English Neighborhood, Bergen County, New Jersey, who settled in Annapolis, Nova Scotia, by 1785. [NA.AO12.16.49]

VAN HORN, NICOLAAS, a pirate in the Caribbean, 1683, 1700. [SPAWI.1683/1163; 1700/953]

VAN HORN, Captain PHILIP, probably in Jamaica, 1782. [HMC.A.III/251]

VAN HORNE, CORNELIUS, in New York, 1723; a Member of the Council of New Jersey, 1727; Mayor of New Jersey, 1736. [SPAWI.1723/606; 1726/377; 1727/579; 1736/402][JCTP.Vol.HH/203][PCCol.1720-1745.833]

VAN HORNE, CORNELIUS GARRET, of New York, husband of Judith, parents of Garret and Augustus Van Horne, probate March 1770 PCC

VAN HORNE, GABRIEL, a Loyalist, formerly of Bergen County, New Jersey, a witness in Fredericton, New Brunswick, 1787. [NA.AO.88/556]

VAN HORNE, GARRIT, a merchant in New York, 1712; 1724. [SPAWI.1712/433; 1724/409]

VAN HORNE, JACOB, in Bergen Neck, New Jersey, 1783. [NA.AO13.87.93]

VAN HORNE, JOHN, a merchant in New York, 1712. [SPAWI.1712/433]

VAN HORNE, JOHN, jr., in Barbados, 1721. [BA.RB6/6399]

VAN HORNE, JOHN, in Bergen Neck, New Jersey, 1783.
[NA.AO13.87.93]

VAN HOUGHNET, MICHAEL, from Johnstown, Tryon
County, New York, a Loyalist and a sergeant of the 2nd
Battalion of the King's Royal Regiment of New York,
settled in Montreal by 1787. [NA.AO12.27.354]

VAN HOUGHNET, WILLIAM, a Loyalist in Johnstown,
Tryon County, New York, 1776. [NA.AO13.80.520]

VAN HOUTEN, HELMUGH, of Bergen, New Jersey, 1783.
[NAS.AO12.110.113]

VAN HOVEN, HENDRICK, a pirate tried in New Providence
in 1699. [SPAWI.1699/928]

VAN ILPENDON, ADRIAN, a Dutch inhabitant of New
York, petitioned the Privy Council in 1668.
[SPAWI.1668.1885]

VAN JANSEN, HENDRICK, in New York, 1690.
[SPAWI.1690/1126]

VAN KIERLEHOVEN, SARAH, in Barbados, 1664.
[BA.RB6/15/456]

VAN KIPP, JOHANNES, in New York, 1699.
[SPAWI.1699/317]

VAN KLEEK, BALTHUS, settled on the Hudson River, New
York, 1697. [see NA.AO12.25.222]

VAN KLEEK, LOWRENS, and his son Leonard, in Dutchess
County, New York, in 1756. [see NA.AO12.25.222]

VAN KLEEK, PETER, husband of Catherina, and parents of
Trintje, Balthus, Leonard, Elizabeth, Sarah, and Peter
Van Kleek, in Dutchess County, New York, around
1750. [see NA.NAO12.25.222]

VAN KLEEK, TRINJE, married Bartholemew Crannell in
1745, settled in Poughkeepsie, Dutchess County, New

York, later in St John, New Brunswick, by 1786.
[NA.AO12.25.222]

VAN LAES, CLAUS LODEWICK, a witness in Barbados,
1668. [see J. Mossier's will probate 6 April 1669
Barbados]

VAN LANG, RICHARD, buried on 21 July 1679 in the parish
of St Michael's, Barbados. [Hotten, p.436]

VAN LIEBERGEN, NICOLAAS, Governor of Curacao,
1679 to 1682. [NWIC#467/145]

VAN LEEUWEN, JACOB, a merchant in the New
Netherlands, 1659. [GAA.NA#1711/521]

VAN LO, PETER, in St Kitts, petitioned for denization in
1662. [SPAWI.1662.269]

VAN LUCCOM, HENRY, emigrated via The Downs,
England, to Barbados on the Falcon in December 1635.
[NA.E157/20]

VAN MAPLE, HENRY, a Loyalist from New York city,
whose widow, Mary, settled in Burton, New Brunswick,
by 1786. [NA.AO12.26.44]

VAN MATER, BENJAMIN, in New Jersey, pre 1776. [see
NA.AO12.14.298]

VAN MATER, CHINEYONCE, son of Joseph Van Mater,
Middletown, Monmouth County, New Jersey, a Loyalist
in 1776, settled in St John, New Brunswick, by 1787.
[NA.AO12.15.340]

VAN MATER, CORNELIUS, in New Jersey, pre 1776.
[NA.AO12.111.57]

VAN MATER, DANIEL, from Freehold, Monmouth County,
New Jersey, a Loyalist in 1776, letters dated 'Bruklen',
1782; in London by 1784, father of Gilbert, Caty, Sarah,
and Micah. [HMC.A.I/386; III/102, 235; IV/64]
[NA.AO12.14.298]

VAN MATER, GILBERT, only son and heir of Daniel Van
Mater in Monmouth County, New Jersey, a Loyalist in
1776, settled on the St John River, New Brunswick.
[NA.AO12.102.78]

VAN MATER, HENRY, from Freehold, New Jersey, a
Loyalist in 1776, in London by 1783.
[HMC.A.I/386][see NA.AO12.14.298; AO12.14.310]

VAN MIDDLESWORTH, ..., in New Jersey, 1750.
[PCCol.1750/485]

VAN NASSAU-SIEGEN, JOHN MAURITS, from Holland
to Brazil in 1636, Governor of Dutch Brazil from 1637 to
1644.

VAN NES, GERRETT, a resident of Albany, New York, in
1700. [SPAWI.1700/845]

VAN NORDEN, GABRIEL, from New Bridge, Bergen
County, New Jersey, a Loyalist in 1776, probably in
New York, 2 April 1780. [HMC.A.II/98]
[NA.AO12.15.237]

VAN OLINDA, DANIEL, a resident of Albany, New York, in
1702.[SPAWI.1702/999]

VAN OLINDA, HELLETIE, an interpreter at Albany, New
York, 20 July 1698. [SPAWI.1698/822i]

VAN OLINDA, JACOB, a resident of Albany, New York, in
1702. [SPAWI.1702/999]

VAN OLINDA, MARTIN, a resident of Albany, New York,
in 1702.[SPAWI.1702/999]

VAN OLINDA, PETER, a resident of Albany, New York, in
1702. [SPAWI.1702/999]

VAN OSDALL, ABRAHAM, in Jamaica, Long Island, New
York, 1783. [NA.AO12.110.165]

VAN PATTEN, ARENT, from Schenectady, Albany County, New York, a Loyalist who settled at Niagara by 1786. [NA.AO13.80.509]

VAN PELL, JAN TOMISON, in Richmond County, New York, 1702. [SPAWI.1702/999]

VAN PERE, ABRAHAM, a Governor of the Dutch West Indies, 1625. [SPCol.1574-1660:105]

VAN PLANK, ISAAC, a resident of Albany, New York, in 1702.[SPAWI.1702/999]

VAN RANST, LUKE, possibly in Nova Scotia, 3 May 1769. [PCCol.1766-1783.194]

VAN RENSSELAER, HENDRICK, Justice of Albany, New York, was suspended in 1699; a resident of Albany in 1702; 1720. [SPAWI.1699/740; 1702/999; 1720/230]

VAN RENSSELAER, JOHN BAPTISTA, naturalised in New York in 1690. [SPAWI.1690/1103]

VAN RENSSALAER, Colonel JOHN, in New York, 1766, 1775. [PCCol.1766/717][JCTP.Vol.82/32]

VAN RENSSALAER, KILLIAN, land grant 4 November 1685; appointed a justice of the peace in Albany, New York, on 27 May 1691, suspended in 1699; a member of the General Assembly of New York, 1699; naturalised before 1695; a resident of Albany in 1702; Commissioner for Indian Affairs, 1708; Colonel in 1718; died 1719.
. [SPAWI.1691/1533; 1699/317, 740; 1702/999; 1708/604. 621] [JCTP.Vols. T/440; W/20] [PCCol.1680-1720.245; 1765/685][NSMA]

VAN RENSSALAER, NICOLAAS, a Dutch Reformed Church minister in New York or Albany, 1674. [SPAWI.1674.1330]

VAN RENSSALAER, RICHARD, petitioned the Privy Council, Colonial, regarding the return of

Renssalaerwyck, 10 January 1695. [PCCol.1680-1720.245]

VAN RENSSALAER, STEPHEN, a letter dated 1791. [NLS.ms3310]

VAN RENSSALAER, STEPHEN, a student from New York in Edinburgh, 1810-1812. [NAS.GD23.6.469]

VAN RUYVEN, CORNELIUS, born in the Netherlands, settled in New Amsterdam, Secretary and Receiver of the New Netherlands, 1664. At Fort James, New York, 1673. [SPAWI.1664.788//1673.1122][NA.HCA. Carteret V. Idle, 1674]

VAN RYAN, JAN, settled on the River Wiapoco with 36 colonists of the Dutch West India Company around 1627. [HS.2nd series, vol.171/271, 336]

VAN RYPER, GARRET, of Bergen, New Jersey, 1783. [NA.AO12.110.25; AO12.110.79]

VAN SCHAACK, ANTHONY, a surgeon and a Loyalist from Albany, New York, in London 1783. [NA.AO12.100.138]

VAN SCHAACK, DAVID, in New York, 7 February 1781. [HMC.A.II/243; IV/452]

VAN SCHAACK, HENRY, an assistant judge before 1776; in New York, 7 February 1781 a letter dated New York, 6 July 1782, later 11 November 1783. [HMC.A.II/243; III/10; IV/452]; in New York 1789. [NA.AO13.87.93; NA.AO12.111.19]

VAN SCHAACK, JOSEPH, in Philadelphia, Pennsylvania, in 1805. [NLS.ms5609/5621]

VAN SCHAACK, PETER, from Kinderhook, Albany County, New York, a lawyer in New York City, a Loyalist in London by 1779. [NA.AO12.101.202]

VAN SCHAICK, GERRET, was appointed as Sheriff of
Albany, New York, in 1719. [SPAWI.1720/48]

VAN SCHAICK, LOVINUS, at Albany, New York, in 1691;
Attorney General of New York, 1692.
[SPAWI.1691/1970;1692/2220]

VAN SCHAYCK, ANNA, in New York, 1701.
[SPAWI.1701/871]

VAN SCHARPHUYSEN, JOHANN, Governor of Surinam
from 1688.

VAN SCHEGAN, JAN, the fiscal of Curacao around 1730.

VAN SCHELLUYNE, CORNELIS, a resident of Albany,
New York, in 1700. [SPAWI.1700/845]

VAN SCHOENHOVEN, DIRK BRADT, in New York, 15
January 1773. [PCCol.1766-1783.358]

VAN SCHONCK, ANTHONY, a resident of Albany, New
York, in 1700. [SPAWI.1700/845]

VAN SCHUILENBURG, PAULUS, Commander of
Demerara from 1767, surrendered the colony to the
British in February 1781. [PCCol.1781/1006]

VAN SEICE, JOHN, an interpreter to Sir William Johnson, at
Onondaga, 6 March 1756. [JCTP.Vol.63/239]

VAN SKEECH, LAURENCE, a resident of Albany, New
York, in 1702.[SPAWI.1702/999]

VAN SKIK, ANTHONY, a resident of Albany, New York, in
1702.[SPAWI.1702/999]

VAN SLEEK, CORNE, a resident of Albany, New York, in
1702.[SPAWI.1702/999]

VAN SLIKE, HARMAN, a resident of Albany, New York, in
1702.[SPAWI.1702/999]

VAN SOLDT, ABRAHAM, in Virginia, son of Mrs Elizabeth Van Soldt probate October 1665 PCC

VAN SOLINGEN, Dr, deceased before 1783, husband of Sarah Van Solingen, in New York, 1783. [NA.AO12.110.13]

VAN SOMMELSDIJK, CORNELIS AERSSEN, born 1637, Governor of Surinam, from 1683. [NWIC]

VAN SPRANG, JAN, master of the Haast U Langzaam at Paramaribo, 1773; master of the Vis at Surinam, 1775. [NWIC]

VAN STAPELS, GELEIN, master of the Flying Drake to Brazil, settled on the Amazon around 1625, later on the Berbice River, returned to the Netherlands, from there to Trinidad, Demerara, and Berbice, in 1629-1630. [RAC#35][HS.2nd series, vol.171/269]

VAN SWIETEN, BEATRIX, sister and executrix of Ouzel Van Swieten, probate July 1705 PCC

VAN SWIETEN, OUZEL in New York, 1698. [SPAWI.1698/593xv]; probate January 1703 and July 1705 PCC

VAN SWERINGEN, GERRIT, from Amsterdam to the Delaware in 1656, in Maryland, 1682; sheriff of St Mary's County, Maryland, 1687; dead by 1700. [SPAWI.1682.380/1674; 1687/1245; 1700/379, 397]

VAN SWERINGEN, JOSEPH and MARY, executors of Garrett Van Sweringen of St Mary's County, Maryland, 1700. [SPAWI.1700/379]

VAN SWERINGEN, Mrs MARY, petitioned the House of Delegates of Maryland in 1699, 1701. [SPAWI.1699/631; 1701/448]

VAN TAARLINGH, FLORIS, a planter in Curacao, 1710.

VAN TASSELL, ABRAHAM, from Croton Bridge, Westchester County, New York, a Loyalist who settled in Digby, Nova Scotia, by 1786. [NA.AO12.110.119]

VAN TASSELL, ISAAC, from Westchester County, New York, a Loyalist who settled in New Brunswick by 1786. [NA.AO1.1.393]

VAN TASSELL, THOMAS, in Westchester County, New York, before 1776. [NA.AO12.110.173]

VAN TEIN, JOHN, a pirate tried in New Providence in 1699. [SPAWI.1699/928]

VAN TEVERE, ANTHONY, in New York on 15 January 1773. [PCCol.1766-1783.358]

VAN THAEK, LOVINUS, an alderman of New York, 1687. [SPAWI.1687/1424]

VAN TIEL, GERRIT SANDERS, residing on the Delaware River, 1664. [SPAWI.1664.808]

VAN TIENHOVEN, CORNELIS, in the New Netherlands, 1624. [GAA.NA#441/155]

VAN TONGERLOO, REYNIER, a privateer in the Caribbean, ca1705.

VAN TRICHT, GERRIT, a merchant in New Amsterdam, the New Netherlands, 1660s. [GAA.NA.3492/167]

VAN TWILLER, GUALTER, at Fort Amsterdam, Governor of the New Netherlands, 1633. [SPCol.1574-1660:171]

VAN TUYLE, DENNIS, an affidavit dated 19 September 1783, New York. [HMC.A.IV/377]

VAN TYLE, MICHAEL, of Bergen Point, New Jersey, 1783. [NA.AO12.110.103]

VAN VEGHTEN, JOHN, Major of the New York Provincials, died at Havanna, husband of Annatje Veghten, probate April 1764 PCC

VAN VEIGHTEN, JOHN, at Albany, New York, in 1702. [SPAWI.1702/387]

VAN VELSIE, or VAN VELSIN, Captain GARRATT, in South Carolina, 1722; 1723; granted 420 acres in Berkley County, SC, on 12 August 1737. [SPAWI.1723/558] [JCTP.Vol.Z/104][NA.CO5.398]

VAN VERT, ISRAEL, in Westchester, New York, before 1776. [NA.AO12.111.9]

VAN VIECHTER or VECHTA, JOHANNES, a resident of Albany, New York, in 1702, 1703.[SPAWI.1702/999; 1703/620]

VAN VIEGHT, DERICK, a resident of Albany, New York, in 1702.[SPAWI.1702/999]

VAN VIOHTEN, FALCOT, a resident of Albany, New York, in 1702.[SPAWI.1702/999]

VAN VLECK, ABRAHAM, in New York, 1731, co-owner of the sloop <u>Two Brothers</u> which was captured off Carolina by the Spanish on 22 August 1727. [SPAWI.1731/94]

VAN VLECQ, ISAAC, an alderman in New York, 1685, 1687. [SPAWI.1685/186;1687/1250]

VAN VOORST, AURY, from Barbados Neck, Bergen County, New Jersey, a Loyalist who settled in Shelburne, Nova Scotia, by 1786. [NA.AO13.25.492]

VAN VORST, GILES, a resident of Albany, New York, in 1702.[SPAWI.1702/999]

VAN VORST, SIMON, indicted and tried on a charge of piracy, in Boston, New England, on 18 October 1717 and found guilty. [SPAWI.1718/575]

VAN VORST, WALLING, of Bergen County, New Jersey, 1783. [NA.AO12.110.163]

VAN VREEDENBURGH, ABRAHAM, Governor of Surinam, around 1690.

VAN WAGGENER, JACOB, in Bergen Neck, New Jersey, 1783. [NA.AO13.87.93]

VAN WART, JACOB, from Cortlandt's Manor, Westchester County, New York, a Loyalist who settled in St John, New Brunswick, by 1786. [NA.AO12.26.17]

VAN WEESP, GIJSBERT CORNELISZOON, a soldier in Brazil 1636, then in Curacao by 1638, finally to the New Netherlands as an innkeeper at Rensslaurwyck by 1664. [GAA.NA.1303/124; NA.1349/42]

VAN WERT, JOHN, an overseer on Colonel William Bayard's plantation before 1776, later by 1786 in Shelburne, Nova Scotia. [NA.AO13.25.499]

VAN WYCK, JOHANES, naturalised in New York, 1735. [SPAWI.1735.591]

VAN ZANT, JOHAN, a resident of New York, 1702, 1719. [SPAWI.1702/1206][JCTP.Vol.V/221]

VAN ZANT, WYNANT, in New York, 1778, 1783. [HMC.A.I/186; III/341, 365]

VATER, ADAM, formerly of Haverstraw, Orange County, New York, but in New York by 1783. [see NA.AO13.16.145]

VEDDER, ARENT, a resident of Albany, New York, in 1702.[SPAWI.1702/999]

VEDDER, CURSET, a resident of Albany, New York, in 1702.[SPAWI.1702/999]

VEDDER, HERMAN, a Dutch inhabitant of New York,
petitioned the Privy Council in 1668.
[SPAWI.1668.1885]

VEDDER, HARMEN, witness to a contract made with the
Mohawk Indians at Schenectady, New York, on 26
December 1700; a resident of Albany, New York, in
1702. [SPAWI.1701/38; 1702/999]

VEGHTE, GERRIT, a member of the General Assembly of
New York, 1699; petitioned the Council of New York,
1699; member of the House of Representatives of New
York, 1701. [SPAWI.1699/317; 1700/416; 1701/1117]

VEMPE, BARENT, in Albany County, New York, 1691.
[SPAWI.1691/1865]

VENES, JAN, a resident of Albany, New York, in
1702.[SPAWI.1702/999]

VERBURGT, FORTIUS, a Dutch Reformed Church minister
on St Croix, Danish West Indies, 1746. [RAK.WIC.429]

VERCHILD, JAMES, proposed as a councillor of St Kitts,
1747. [JCTP.Vol.59/67]

VERCHILD, JASPER, a planter in St Kitts, 1712.
[JCTP.Vol.P/229]

VERCHILD, PHILIP, a planter in St Kitts, 1712.
[JCTP.Vol.P/243]

VERHOF, Father, a Catholic priest on Curacao, 1750s?

VERKUYL, NICOLAAS, a Dutch Reformed Church minister
on Curacao from 1679 to his death in 1713.

VERLETT, NICHOLAS, in the New Netherlands, 1664.
[SPAWI.1664.788]

VERMILSE, JOHANNES, in New York, 1689.
[SPAWI.1689/217]

VERMUILLEN, JOHANNES, was pardoned by the Privy Council, Colonial, on 7 April 1692. [PCCol.1680-1720.204]

VERPLANCK, HAAC, a resident of Albany, New York, in 1700. [SPAWI.1700/845]

VERSCHUUR, JOHANNES, master of the Vertrouwen at Surinam, 1791. [NWIC]

VIELIE, MYNDERT, born 1706, a farmer, with his wife, born 1716, Loyalist refugees in New York, 1778. [HMC.A.I/345]

VIELLE, ARNOUT CORNELIS, an interpreter at Albany, New York, 20 July 1698, 1699. [SPAWI.1698/822i]; 1699/250

VIELLE, CORNELIS, a resident of New York, 1702. [SPAWI.1702/1206]

VIELLE, GARRET, in New York, 1700.[SPAWI.1700/909]

VIELLE, GARRET, from Rensselaer, Albany County, New York, a Loyalist who settled in Quebec by 1786. [NA.AO13.16.206]

VOLCKERSON, IMMETGE, a resident of New York or Albany, then in Amsterdam, successfully petitioned King Charles II for permission to return to New York from Amsterdam aboard the Fort Albany of New York in 1669. [SPAWI.1669.29]

VOLLE, JACOB, at Fort Kijkoveral, Essequibo, 1702. [SPAWI.1702/699]

VON BRUNNEN, ARNOLD, a Dutch Reformed Church minister on St Thomas, Danish West Indies, 1735. [RAK.WIC.431]

VON SPORCKE, Baron, Governor of Surinam, died 1752. [NWIC#288]

VON WYNGARDE, JOHAN LUDOVICK, a Dutch
Reformed Church minister in the Danish West Indies,
1748. [RAK.WIC.429]

VOORHEES, HENDRICK, of Hackensack, New Jersey,
1783. [NA.AO12.110.33]

VORKIRK, PETER, in Bergen Neck, New Jersey, 1783.
[NA.AO13.87.93]

VORSTERRE, P., Governor of Surinam, 1672.
[SPAWI.1672/920/1336/1355/1367/1380/1384/1401]

VREELANDT, GEORGE, in Bergen Neck, New Jersey,
1783. [NA.AO13.87.93]

VREELANDT, JOHN, in Bergen Neck, New Jersey, 1783.
[NA.AO13.87.93; AO12.111.3]

VREELANDT, MICHAEL, in Bergen Neck, New Jersey,
1783. [NA.AO13.87.93]

VRELANT, CORNELIUS, of Bergen, New Jersey, 1783.
[NA.AO12.110.19]

VROOM, JOHN, formerly a farmer in Middlesex County,
New Jersey, later by 1784 in Annapolis, Nova Scotia.
[NA.AO13.21.432]

VROOM, PETER, formerly a farmer in Middlesex County,
New Jersey, later by 1784 in Annapolis, Nova Scotia.
[NA.AO13.21.432]

VROOMAN, ADAM, witness to a contract made with the
Mohawk Indians at Schenectady, New York, on 26
December 1700; a resident of Albany in 1702.
[SPAWI.1701/38; 1702/999]

VROOMAN, PETER, a resident of Albany, New York, in
1702.[SPAWI.1702/999]

WAGER, EVERARD, of Rensselaer Manor, Albany County,
New York, 1783. [NA.AO13.16.263]

WALDRON, RUTGART, possibly a tradesman at Fort
William Henry, New York, in 1702. [SPAWI.1702/387]

WAUGELDER, HARMANUS, an Alderman of New York,
1727. [SPAWI.1727/763v]

WEDDERLIN, JOHANIS, naturalised in New York, 1735.
[SPAWI.XLI.591]

WEEJAR, EVERHART, in Filstown, Albany County, New
York, 1786. [NA.AO12.33.71]

WEEJAR, JACOB, formerly in Cocksburgh, Albany County,
New York, a Loyalist who settled on the Bay of Quinte,
Canada, by 1786. [NA.AO12.29.10]

WEITBECK, FOLGERT, a resident of Albany, New York, in
1702.[SPAWI.1702/999]

WELIUS, EVERARD, a minister, who died in the New
Netherlands in 1659.[GAA.NA#3613/237]

WENDELL, ABRAHAM, an Indian trader in the Sinnekes
country, New York, 1730. [SPAWI.1730/622]

WENDELL, EVERT, a resident of Albany, New York, in
1700; a Commissioner of Indian Affairs of New York, at
Albany in 1730. [SPAWI.1700/845; 1730/622]

WENDELL, HARMANUS, a resident of Albany, New York,
in 1700; 1720. [SPAWI.1700.845; 1720/230]

WESSELS, DIRICK, Recorder of New York, 1687, 1691;
resigned his share of Mohawk lands on 19 April 1698; a
Justice of the Peace and resident of Albany in 1700;
Representative for the City and County of Albany, 1701;
witnessed a contract with the Five Nations in Albany on
19 July 1701; a resident of Albany in 1702; Colonel in
1718. [SPAWI.1687/1424; 1691/1610; 1700/845;
1701/754, 758; 1702/999][JCTP.Vol.T/440]
[PCCol.1707/182]

WESTERVELT, DOWER, of Bergen, New Jersey, 1783. [NA.AO12.110.83]

WESTERVELT, JOHN, of Bergen, New Jersey, 1783. [NA.AO12.110.83]

WESTERVELT, ROCLOFF, of Bergen, New Jersey, 1783. [NA.AO12.110.83]

WICKOST, CLAUS, in King's County, Nassau Island, New York, 1702. [SPAWI.1702/999]

WILDRIK, RUDOLFUS, a Dutch Reformed Church minister in Curacao from 1758 to 1765, then in St Eustatius, died in Curacao in 1794.

WILLEKENS, JACOB, Admiral of a Dutch fleet that arrived at Salvador da Bahia in May 1624.

WILLEMS, JACOB, a memorial re events in New York between 1690 and 1691, dated Amsterdam, 15 October 1691. [SPAWI.1691.1840]

WILLEMS, HANS JURGEN, a soldier sent from the Netherlands to Essequibo in 1700. [SPAWI.1700/715]

WINCOOP, Justice, in Ulster County, New York, 1695. [SPAWI.1699/292]

WINKLER, HERMAN, at Fort Kykoverall, Rio Essequibo, 1718. [SPAWI.1718/690, 693]

WINNE, LIVINIUS, a resident of Albany, New York, in 1700. [SPAWI.1700/845]

WITBECK, JAN, a resident of Albany, New York, in 1702.[SPAWI.1702/999]

WITT, BARENT, in New York, 1689. [SPAWI.1689/352]

WITT, JAMIETIDE, a Dutch inhabitant of New York, petitioned the Privy Council in 1668. [SPAWI.1668.1885]

WYNANT, DANIEL, in New York, 1783. [NA.AO12.111.59]

WYNANT, GEORGE, in New Jersey, 1783.
[NA.AO12.110.79]

WYNIA, DIRCK, master of the <u>Watervliet</u> at Surinam, 1745.
[NWIC]

WYNKOOP, BENJAMIN, in New York, 1723.
[SPAWI.1723/606]

ZELL, CHRISTOFFEL, master of the <u>Zeemercuur</u> at
Surinam, 1793. [NWIC]

CPSIA information can be obtained
at www.ICGtesting.com
Printed in the USA
FSOW04n1444080915
10827FS